Optimism Is a Choice

And other timeless ideas

Moshe Cohen

Copyright © 2021 by Moshe Cohen

All rights reserved. No part of this publication may be reproduced, distributed, or transmitted in any form or by any means, including photocopying, recording, or other electronic or mechanical methods, without the prior written permission of the publisher, except in the case of brief quotations embodied in critical reviews and certain other noncommercial uses permitted by copyright law.

ISBN: 978-1-7352600-2-0 (paperback)
ISBN: 978-1- 7352600-3-7 (ebook)
Library of Congress Control Number: 2021923997

Front cover design by Harini Rajagopalan.
Front cover image by Peyman Farmani from Unsplash.com.
Front cover image by Ritam Baishya from Unsplash.com.
Front cover icon by Aleksander Vector from The Noun Project.
Book design by Harini Rajagopalan.
www.harini-rajagopalan.squarespace.com

First printing edition 2021.

The Negotiating Table, Inc.
1089, Commonwealth Avenue #354
Boston, MA 02115
www.neotiatingtable.com

Acknowledgments

I'm an optimist by choice, but didn't get there on my own. I've had numerous family members, teachers, friends, and others inspire me to take an optimistic approach to things. It would be difficult to list everyone, so I'll just call out a few.

My mother, Aviva Wertheim Cohen, faced challenges and hardship with a determined smile, always encouraging me to look for the positives and to embrace possibilities. My grandmothers, Miriam Simon Wertheim and Bracha Cohen braved difficult times with grace and hope, finding joy in the little moments. My father, Hanania Cohen, and sister, Iris Cohen Fineberg, always make me feel like anything is possible, offering support and encouragement through challenges and helping me celebrate successes.

I would be nowhere without my amazing wife, Barbra Batshalom, who brings out the best in me, and my wonderful children, Maya, Ariel, Elan, and Nadav, who inspire and motivate me every day.

A special thanks to Ryan Orr, a wonderful teacher, editor, and writer, who edited the manuscript, and to Jenna Winkler, who took a thoughtful second pass at it. I also want to call out Scott Taylor, whose leadership class at Boston University's Questrom School of Business introduced me to the idea that optimism is a choice. Thanks also to Catie Hutchings, for demonstrating optimism as a practice, and to Irina Navarro, for helping me think through different ways of representing my ideas.

Thank you to Harini Rajagopalan, for the inspired ideas, creative designs, and diligent effort that led to the look and feel of the book, inside and out, and for putting up with my endless changes.

Finally, thanks to the many teachers, colleagues, family members, friends, clients, and especially students, from whom I learn every day and who foster the environment in which these ideas sprouted and grew. I'm grateful to have learned from you.

Contents

Introduction	9
Optimism is a Choice	12
The Power of Letting Go	14
Finding Joy in the Gloom	16
The Invisible Cocoon	18
Heroes in Small Ways	20
Smart and Lucky	22
Question Everything	24
Humbled and Connected	26
Patience and Perseverance	28
Uncertainty	30
Reach Out Across the Divide	32
Hope, Fear and Opportunity	34
Do Something, Anything	36
Summer is Here!	38
Information, Beliefs, and Conclusions	40
Setbacks Happen	42
Life is Good	44
Negotiating in a Pandemic	46
Victory Lap	48

If We Don't Ask	50
Fear of Conflict	52
Once Upon a Time	54
Deal or No Deal?	56
Get Lost!	58
What is in the Way?	60
Life is Short	62
Bad Things Happen	64
Feeling Powerless	66
Out of Our Minds	68
Overwhelmed	70
Yes, We Can	72
The "Uch" Factor	74
Do Something Crazy	76
Everything is Conversation	78
No Easy Answers	80
Life Changing Moments	82
The Marshmallow Test	84
Beyond Marshmallows	86
Every Day	88
Time	90
Resistance to Change	92

Gratitude	94
Happy New Year	96
Curiosity	98
Words Without Consequences	100
Take the Day Off	102
Too Much Bad News	104
A Light in the Distance	106
Judgment Day	108
Lessons from the Weather	110
Jethro the Consultant	112
Milestones	114
Both And	116
The Optimistic Lifestyle	118
The Causality Calamity	120
Thriller	122
Fifteen Years	124
Prisoners of Our Nature	126
Anxiety Time	128
Willpower	130
After the Apocalypse	132
Concluding Thoughts	134
Index	135

Introduction

In March of 2020, we went into lockdown. Businesses tried to figure out how to operate remotely, schools closed for a time, and then tried to manage in various ways, loved ones became separated, or conversely, got cooped up together in isolation. Over the next fourteen months, we learned to function differently, connect virtually, exercise at home, cook in our own kitchens, and watch even more TV than before. We adapted, as humans do, to changes in the environment, and developed coping strategies that served us in various ways.

But not everyone had the luxury of shopping online, ordering dinner, and binge-watching old TV series. First responders and medical workers faced the pandemic head-on, caring for the sick, watching people die, and putting themselves in harm's way every day. Others made it possible for the rest of the population to live remotely, making things in factories, working at warehouses and stores, driving and delivering goods, cleaning and disinfecting facilities, educating our children, and caring for our elders. They, too, were on the front line, though often taken for granted or ignored.

At first, an eerie quiet settled over the land. Traffic disappeared from our highways, people avoided leaving their homes, and many people barely connected with friends and family. As the pandemic evolved, so did our responses. Things became heated, and regional, political, social, and other divisions appeared. Some locations stayed locked down, while others opened up, only to lock down again. People debated about masks, vaccines, closures, schools, with some even questioning whether the pandemic was real, while others questioned their sanity. Rifts developed, as polarized points of view caused friendships to falter and family members to stop speaking to each other.

Throughout it all, the medical community kept taking care of the sick, learning more about the disease, and developing more effective strategies to treat it. Biopharma organizations throughout the world developed a set of safe, effective vaccines in record time, starting to vaccinate the general population within about a year of the outbreak. As winter turned to spring, and a significant portion of the vulnerable population became vaccinated, restrictions started to loosen. First, we no longer needed masks outdoors, then with family, and then in larger crowds. Very quickly, we went from living under siege to feeling strangely normal. While the pandemic hadn't ended, and the danger had not completely passed, people started returning to work, seeing friends, dining out, and going to movies.

From the beginning of the lockdown, I started writing weekly articles to raise my own spirits and help me get through the time. I shared those articles with others, hoping it would help them as well. The topics were random, based on my thoughts at the moment of writing, but the response was exciting. It was a tough year for many people, and I was glad to see that there was something I could do to help people manage. I wrote sixty-one articles in all, each only a three-minute read. The first, titled Optimism is a Choice, reminds us that there is a difference between what happens to us, and how we respond to what happens. The final article, called After the Apocalypse, celebrates the end of the pandemic while voicing a cautionary note for the future.

I've collected these articles into this volume to help people remember key moments from the pandemic and learn lessons for the future. They include thoughts about optimism, mindfulness, negotiation, decision-making, attitude, and many other topics. While the articles capture moments in time, their messages are often timeless, providing ideas to help us manage our lives, both in good times and during crises. I hope they provide you with interesting and useful thoughts and help you as well.

Chapter 1

Optimism is a Choice

March 21

> *The Roman god Janus had two faces, one looking forward to the future and one looking back to the past. We don't. We only have one face and must choose where to look. Where are you looking?*

These are challenging times. With a pandemic shutting down the world, separating us from each other, and threating our livelihoods, it's easy to despair. The news gets worse from day to day, the choices more difficult, the anxiety deepens, and it's hard to imagine a time when we won't be terrified for our lives, our health, our loved ones, and our ability to get by.

But especially in dark times like these, it's more important than ever to remember that optimism is a choice. Whatever our circumstances, no matter how dire, even if everything else is taken away from us, the thing we can hold onto is our internal response. This is not a new idea. Viktor Frankl and others have said it before me. But when times get tough, it's easy to forget and difficult to hold onto hope and a positive attitude, so I thought a reminder might be helpful.

Optimism does not mean putting our heads in the sand and pretending that things aren't as bad as they are. It does not involve hanging on to false hopes and imaginary solutions. Optimism is the act of staring at terrible odds, knowing that the chance of redemption are small, and believing that with a positive attitude and effort, it's possible to get there. Optimism means not giving into despair, never giving up, and taking things one moment at a time, preparing for the worst, and hoping for the best.

Our optimism will be challenged constantly over the next days, weeks, and months. We will encounter setbacks and terrifying moments and it will be difficult to stay positive in the face of bad news and fear. We will need help from each other to keep going in these frightening times, and despite that, we will have bad days when hope eludes us. But we need to get back there. Optimism needs to be our choice because all other choices are worse, and because there might be times when it is all we've got.

My wish for all of us is that we can hold onto this choice, to stay optimistic when we can, and get back to positive thinking after our setbacks. I hope we reach out to those around us and help them in their moments of dejection and that we ask for support when we need others to help revive our spirits. Optimism is a choice – not an easy choice, but in my mind, the only one we can afford as we socially distance, wash our hands, and try to figure out a way forward.

Chapter 2

The Power of Letting Go

March 28

> *Realizing that reality often turns out very differently than we had planned is either disappointing or wonderful, depending on how we choose to view things.*

It's hard not to be frightened! More bad news comes out each day. We are fearful for our health, our loved ones, our livelihoods, and our future. We live in isolation, our routines have been upended, our plans have been dashed, and there is no clear end in sight. We feel lost, helpless, dismayed at having lost control over our lives, and as time drags on, increasingly anxious. Like Frodo, in The Lord of the Rings, we "wish none of this had happened."

But there is some solace in Gandalf's response: "So do all who live to see such times, but that is not for them to decide. All we have to decide is what to do with the time that is given to us." Similarly, in The Seven Habits of Highly Effective People, Stephen Covey distinguishes between our Circle of Concern – the things we care about, and our Circle of Influence – the things we can do something about. We can reclaim power in our lives by identifying what we can influence, and even more importantly, by letting go where we have no control.

There's a virus spreading throughout the world. People are getting sick, and some are dying. The world economy has largely shut down. Politicians and policymakers are making decisions and uttering declarations, some wise and others ineffective or even damaging. Billions of people are now hunkering down, confined to their homes, unable to work or study. There is currently no cure, no vaccine, and no clear end in sight. That is our world today, and for most of us, all of that is out of our control.

But we can choose to let all of that go. Looking at the news every hour to get an update on the number of people stricken by the virus only increases our anxiety. Getting upset with what our politicians are saying or with the choices other people are making just makes us miserable. Wishing for a miracle cure or pretending things aren't as bad as they are doesn't change reality. The way to gain power is to acknowledge that we control none of those things, let them go, and focus on the little things.

What can we learn today? What can we create? How can we help someone else? Who can we connect with? Who can we call who might be even lonelier? What small nuggets of opportunity can we find amid the ruins? How often can we laugh? Our power comes from letting go. By focusing on what we can do rather than lamenting what we can't control, we can make small improvements to our own lives and be a positive force to those around us.

Chapter 3

Finding Joy in the Gloom

April 4

> *Sometimes when we admire the mountains on the horizon, we miss the flowers blooming by the side of the path.*

It's been a gloomy week – cloudy, rainy, chilly, windy, gray, and on top of that, the whole world seems to have shut down, menaced by the Coronavirus. Our routines have been disrupted, our finances are in disarray, we are isolated from our friends and loved ones, shut out of our normal places, and have no idea how bad it will get or for how long. It's been gloomy for a while, weeks for some, months for others, and looking out into the future, more dismal weeks and months might await us. As the fog envelops us, it's hard not to sink into a sad, anxious, helpless, and seemingly endless despair.

In the gloom, we await the dawn, and it will arrive, eventually; the clouds will part, and the sun will peak through. But we can't afford to succumb to the darkness without reaching for the light, finding joy in the little things, and cracking a smile once in a while. Albert Camus wrote, "In the midst of winter, I found there was, within me, an invincible summer. And that makes me happy. For it says that no matter how hard the world pushes against me, within me, there's something stronger – something better, pushing right back."

It is up to us to find joy within difficult times - to notice that the leaves are starting to turn green, and that flowers are starting to poke out of the ground. It is our choice to appreciate the moments of closeness that we can find in the time cooped up together or conversely by connecting remotely with friends and family far away. It is by decision that we can find bits of humor within the many tragedies unfolding around us.

Looking for moments of happiness and finding glimmers of joy within the gloom doesn't diminish the terrible impacts of the virus nor does it change the trajectory of how bad things might get. But by focusing on joy we can dramatically change our experience of the situation, however miserable it might become. We give ourselves a gift, and we spread that gift to those around us.

We can start with the little things – the funny face someone made on Zoom, the crazy cat chasing a shadow on the wall, the meme that someone sent and made us smile. We can appreciate the joy of slowing down, the wonder of the silence around us, the beauty of our streets with all of the cars and people gone. We can rejoice in the laughter of a child, a wag of a tail, a wave from a neighbor, an old photograph, a favorite rerun, or a random thought. Dawn will come, but we mustn't wait to find the light within and all around us.

Chapter 4

The Invisible Cocoon

April 11

> *When the music stops, and the party has ended, when the guests have all left and the lights are back on, someone has to muster the energy to clean up the mess that has been left behind.*

Social distancing is uncomfortable. We sit alone, connect remotely, isolated from family and friends, and driven away from the places we like to go. We can't eat at restaurants, shop at stores, visit the theater, go to the beach, have dinner with friends, or see colleagues at the office. Trapped in our homes, we languish in our loneliness, chafe against the isolation, stare out the window resentfully at the birds that still flock together, and complain that this is going on for too long.

All of the discomfort we feel is valid, and all of our complaints are warranted. We have been torn away from our lives, forced to learn new technologies and adopt new routines, and must stare at the same walls every day. We worry about money and the economy, and live with the terrible fear that we or people we care about might get sick. The loneliness can be crushing, the uncertainty anxiety-provoking, and there is no end in sight.

But we are privileged to be able to socially distance in this way. The lights in our houses are on, the internet is working, water flows through our taps, and the stove still lights. We can get our food delivered and our trash removed. Work and school have miraculously moved online, our cellphones and computers connect us with the world, and the walls we resent protect us from the cold. Police and firefighters still come when we need them, and on the front lines, paramedics, nurses, doctors, and other medical professionals take care of the sick.

There is an invisible cocoon that shelters us and allows us to continue our lives in isolation. The people who grow our food, harvest it, package it, deliver it to stores, stock the shelves, select it, pack it, and drive it to our doors can't socially isolate and protect themselves as we do, the final recipients of the goods. When we buy something online, we need to remember that someone built it, assembled it, shipped it, and got it to our door. People are working crazy hours to keep our utilities running, to manage the infrastructure so we can connect remotely, and to take care of us.

We need to appreciate the people who can't self-isolate, who put themselves in harm's way so we can socially distance and complain. Most of these people are invisible to us, unknown and unseen, and even those we see, running our stores, delivering our packages, removing our recycling, and taking care of the sick and dying, we barely notice. So, this is a shout out to the invisible cocoon, to the ones who get together and put themselves at risk so we can stay apart, and so that society can beat this virus and see happier days.

Chapter 5

Heroes in Small Ways

April 17

> *Sometimes, when you are feeling lost, the best distraction from your own troubles is to help someone else with theirs. In the words of Gandhi, "The best way to find yourself is to lose yourself in the service of others."*

A pandemic naturally makes us feel helpless, trapped in our homes, unable to engage in our most mundane routines, anxious over everything, and increasingly desperate, not knowing when it will end. We look for heroes to rescue us. We expect our national and local leaders to enact policies that fix everything, hope our scientists and doctors will find miracle cures and vaccines to keep us safe, and look for salvation from our community or religious institutions. Powerless to help ourselves, we peer out the window and gaze at our screens, praying for superheroes to swoop in and save the day.

But we are not as helpless as we think, and strangely, our power is greatest when we focus on helping those around us rather than ourselves. We can be heroes in small ways, by reaching out to others, lending a hand where we can, making other people's lives a little better, and simply showing that we care. As we look around, we see signs of heroism all around us, from people sewing masks for medical workers, to checking in on neighbors, to caring for children so that others can work.

There is so much we can do without ever leaving our homes. We can alleviate someone else's loneliness by calling them and listening to their concerns. We can read stories to kids in far-away places to give their parents a moment of peace to get something done. We can check in on our neighbors to make sure that they have food and to ask how we can help them. We can create something beautiful or funny and share it with the world, to help lighten other people's spirits. We can start small.

By helping others, we help ourselves even more. We shift our focus away from our fear, anxiety and helplessness, and regain the power that comes with doing. We do best when we develop a mindset of service, look for ways to make other people's lives a little better, and take action. Let's face it – our minds aren't fun places to be right now. We are bored, lonely, anxious, scared, and helpless. But there is a whole world of need around us, creating opportunities for us to focus outward rather than just inward, and to do well by doing good.

Our power as a species comes not from the prowess or wisdom of individuals, but from the collaborative network of people helping people to strengthen the collective. While we need our policy-makers, scientists, doctors, and spiritual leaders to do their best, we can't afford to wait for the superheroes to come save us. Instead, we need to look around, focus our awareness on the little things we can do to help others, and start doing them. We can be the heroes in small ways, and in saving others, empower and save ourselves.

Chapter 6

Smart and Lucky

April 25

> *If you believe that you are lucky, you're more likely to be lucky. "Always look for parking by the door of your destination - you're just as likely to find it there as elsewhere."* - Hanania Cohen (my Dad)

In this time of peril, there are no clear choices. Do we stay locked in our homes or venture outside? Do we keep our economy shuttered or risk opening it up? How do we grapple with unemployment, bankruptcy, and hunger while also minimizing infection, illness, and death? Are we being too cautious, too complacent? How do we keep safe? How do we keep sane? How do we know what to do?

As always, we can only make the best decisions we can based on the information available to us. We have to be smart, since the wrong choices can be damaging or even fatal, but how do we assess risks and make sound decisions? In Thinking Fast and Slow, Daniel Kahneman asserts that our minds operate on two levels – our intuitive and emotional mind makes most of the decisions while getting occasional guidance from the rational and data-driven part. As a result, we might make terrible choices.

We therefore need to slow down and ask hard questions, to be skeptical of simple solutions, tempting as they might be, and push back when we think we have clear answers. We need to take decisive action, but based on sound data from a variety of sources, input and ideas from a diverse set of people, and careful analysis of possible outcomes. We face murky choices every day, and we can't wait for perfect information before deciding, but we also can't be impulsive and rely on our gut. We need to be smart.

There are no guarantees. We can choose wisely but end up getting hurt. We can mess up and have things can turn out fine. There are heavy smokers who live to be one hundred and healthy joggers who die before their time. Life is statistical, and that's scary, because we have no real control, but it's also encouraging, because both bad and good things might happen. In the movie, Chicken Run, Bunty, one of the chickens trying to escape from the farm, says to Ginger, the ringleader, "The chances of us getting out of here are a million to one." Ginger replies, "Then there's still a chance." In the end, the results can go either way, and it's a game of odds.

Although we are always rolling the dice, our choices do matter as we try to improve the odds in our favor. We decide what ideas to support, what actions to take, and how to interact with others. We try to consider the odds and question whether we are making them better or worse. In the end, we have to be smart and we have to be lucky, since the less smart we are, the luckier we need to be. It's tough! There are no simple answers. We make the best choices we can, accept uncertainty, and hope for the best.

Chapter 7

Question Everything

May 2

> *We fear the unknown because we imagine something dangerous around the bend, but we might instead find new opportunities, amazing wonders, and enchanting discoveries as well.*

Our world has come to a screeching halt. Everything is different now. If we still have work at all, it's not the same as it was. We work from home, meet people virtually, hope our devices and our internet are up to the task. We stare day after day at the same four walls, cut off from our friends, banished from our coffee shops, torn away from our routines. We don't drive, because there is nowhere to go, don't shop because the stores are closed, don't eat out or see movies. Our schedules have been upended, our activities diminished, and our choices curtailed.

At this time, it's natural to feel a yearning for things to go back to where they were, to our jobs, our routines, and our freedoms. Trapped at home, we long to return to work and for our kids to go back to school. We miss our Starbucks and trips to the mall. We long to get back on planes and trains, to see friends and go to restaurants, and maybe the gym. Sidelined at home, we miss our old lives and hope things get back to normal soon.

But in life, we can never go back, only forward. Like every

epidemic before it, this one will pass eventually, and we will emerge from our homes. The world will get back to normal, but what that means is an open question. The "normal" we were used to before the epidemic left a lot to be desired. As we wait out the virus to run its course, we therefore have the opportunity to question everything and possibly to design a better future.

Do we really miss those three-hour commutes? Will we really miss twelve-hour days at work or petty office politics? Do we really need everything we bought before, racking up bills and filling our houses with junk we had to either store or get rid of? We were on a treadmill running ever faster and never stopping to think, racing through our days and ticking items off lists, and in our rush to entertain ourselves, forgot how to enjoy life.

The virus brings illness and death, as well as hardship and misery. We all long for it to pass. But while we are stuck in lockdown, forced to slow down, we finally have a moment to examine our priorities. How have our choices measured up to our values? What narratives were we telling ourselves, and what paradigms were we stuck in? Can we make different choices going forward to create a cleaner, kinder, and better world? What can we learn from this experience? What do we really want? By questioning everything, we can emerge from the pandemic into a new, improved reality for ourselves and those around us.

Chapter 8

Humbled and Connected

May 11

> *When I feel anxious, I think about the depths of the ocean, the vastness of the galaxy, the countless generations that have preceded me, the number of atoms in a single grain of sand, the seeming endlessness of the universe, and suddenly, my problems don't seem so important any more.*

Over the past seventy thousand years, humanity has transformed into the dominant life form on the planet. Every day, our numbers grow, we take over more habitats, and develop greater capabilities. We reach beyond Earth, aim to colonize other planets, and send our spacecraft into inter-stellar space. We create technologies, uncover the mysteries of the genome, increase our lifespans through medical advances, and write algorithms that leverage and transcend our intelligence. We think very highly of ourselves!

And then, one day, a microscopic virus comes along and knocks us to the ground. Millions get infected, hundreds of thousands die, and the rest of us sit locked down in our homes. Our economies disintegrate overnight, social and political orders are upended, global collaboration becomes strained, and our lifestyles vanish before our eyes. We are humbled, and not by a large asteroid, but by a microscopic pathogen.

But around us, the Earth seems fine. Seasons come and go,

the moon waxes and wanes, and the sun shines brightly. In The World Without Us, Alan Wiseman examines what would happen to the natural and built environment if humans suddenly ceased to exist. While we are still here, and despite the virus, our numbers are still growing, our footprint has temporarily shrunk. We stay home, and even when we do venture out, we do so in smaller numbers and for a shorter time.

Weeds grow through the cracks of unused parking lots, and tree roots crack our sidewalks. Wildlife, so often pushed out of its natural habitats and driven to near extinction by our actions, makes a comeback. Foxes and wild boars invade our cities, flamingoes flourish in urban parks, all manner of reptiles and insects venture nearer to our homes. The air above our cities clears, waterways become less polluted, and a hush settles over our homes.

At this time, it has become obvious that despite our advances, we are not above the natural world but a part of it. We are connected to the other species that surround us, to the resources we exploit, and to each other. In order to recover, survive, and flourish, we need to harness our ability to collaborate with each other and solve the big problems together. Now more than ever, we need to think holistically and avoid gravitating to short-term fixes, partisan divisions, and wishful thinking.

We are down but not out. The pandemic will subside, and we will hopefully find both medical treatments and vaccines to combat the virus. In time, we will forget how we were humbled and go back to dominating the planet. But this is not the last microbe out there, and somewhere in the skies there might be an asteroid. We are an inventive and over-achieving species, but we are also self-destructive. Only by remaining humble and connected both to each other and to the greater natural world can we recover from the current situation, resume our lives, and manage future challenges effectively.

Chapter 9

Patience and Perseverance

May 18

> *Things don't always go the way we want, and there are challenges and setbacks along the way, but if we persist in stubbornly putting one foot in front of the other, we might find ways to persevere and outlast the difficulties.*

It's been two months since our world ground to a halt, two months of anxiety and uncertainty. Two months is a long time to be working from home, or not at all, to be out of school, or squinting into a computer screen. Two months is a long time to be cut off from friends and family, driven away from the places we love and barred from the things we enjoy. We are losing patience and tired of sitting at home.

If in the beginning, fear of the virus brought us together and helped us comply with social distancing directives, as time wears on our nerves, we increasingly resent and chafe against those same directives. The health advice that made sense to us as the virus spread across the world can now seem misguided as we look at the economic devastation that followed in its wake. We start thinking that the cure might be worse than the disease, and look for people to blame. We agitate to restore our livelihoods, see our friends, and resume our lives.

But outside the door waits the virus, which has already

sickened nearly five million people and has killed over 300,000 in a few short months. Unlike us, the virus is patient, hoping we lower our guard and get near each other. The virus doesn't care what we believe or which news outlets we watch. The virus doesn't mind being called fake news or scoffed at as an exaggeration. It's not even technically alive. Just a bit of genetic material encased in protein, shed from one host, waiting for another host to come along. The logic is pretty simple. If the virus is denied access to new hosts, it dies, while if it keeps finding new hosts to infect, it spreads.

To be effective in our fight against such a mindless and persistent enemy, we too need to be patient and persistent while making difficult choices, with no easy answers or quick solutions. We need to be strategic in our approach, consistent in our actions, and collaborative in our attitude. Someday, hopefully soon, vaccines and treatments will defeat this virus. Until then, we must be vigilant, since we are all possible hosts or victims. While we need to work and feed our families, we must also stay focused on eradicating the virus and protecting ourselves and each other.

But we are an impatient species, and the longer this goes on, the harder it is to be patient and persevere. We focus on the short-term and the local, rather than the long-term and the global. We give up and take reckless risks to our peril. Instead, we need to slow down our reactions and question our impulses. We need to ask for assistance and offer help to others. We can defeat this virus and get back to normal, but to succeed, we need to work together and play the game to its conclusion.

Chapter 10

Uncertainty

May 23

> *In a time of uncertainty and fear, when we tend to dread surprises and equate them with disaster, it is important to remain optimistic and hold out hope that good things will come our way as well.*

Coping with uncertainty can be difficult. We look for answers and crave solutions. Some of our questions are existential. Why are we here? What is the meaning of our lives? Who created all of this? What happens when we die? Why do bad things happen to good people? Lacking facts with which to answer these questions, we rely on beliefs, stories, and our imaginations to generate certainty. We settle for limited, invented explanations because we can't deal with the idea that the answers to some questions might be forever beyond our reach, and that other questions might simply have no answers at all.

We are equally challenged when it comes to moral decisions. At times, we don't know whether to be truthful or kind, or how to balance responsibility and compassion? What do we prioritize? What ethical standards should we apply, and how do we adjust our choices based on time and circumstances? What rules do we set for our societies and how do we respond to infractions of those rules? How do we deal with our own transgressions, and what do we do when the rules give us confusing or conflicting guidance? Ultimately, we want someone to tell us.

Seeking certainty, we look for simple solutions, clear guidelines, and comprehensive rules, and we put our faith in people who promise us these answers. Whether we follow politicians, religious leaders, pundits, or philosophers, we elevate the messengers and stop questioning the message. We believe our trusted information sources without examining the information they present to us. Feeling like they've given us the truth, and we can therefore make decisions, reduces our anxiety and makes us happier, but it can also divide us and lead to unfortunate choices.

It's much tougher to accept uncertainty, to recognize that there are often no clear answers, and in some cases, no answers at all. But if we go there, push through our discomfort and fear, we might find that there is also great wonder in not knowing, in embracing the idea that having the answers might be much less interesting than the process of asking the questions. In asking ever more difficult questions and exploring different avenues to resolve them, we make profound discoveries and develop new ideas.

Without definite answers, our decisions are only educated guesses, our best ideas wrung out through experimentation and vigorous debate. By accepting the idea that we might never know, we avoid the temptation of seeking simplistic truths and open our minds to alternative explanations, conflicting schools of thought, and novel solutions. We build bridges rather than walls, welcome diverse opinions, and no longer feel threatened by those who disagree with us. Uncertainty is anxiety-provoking, but without it we are diminished, shutting our eyes, while a vast universe of unanswerable questions lies before us, waiting to be explored.

Chapter 11

Reach Out Across the Divide

June 1

> *Amid the chaos and difficulties of these times, if we pause to notice the uncountable acts of kindness performed by people every day, it's hard not to feel hopeful for the future.*

Feeling stressed? With the pandemic, economic uncertainty, and social and political turmoil, it's easy to feel anxious. We feel isolated, and our connection with others is virtual, or when in person, limited to a small set of people around us. In this environment, it is normal to feel sad and lonely with the isolation, helpless and frustrated, and angry at the people who are supposed to be helping us out of this mess. It is also natural to become insular, stay within our echo chambers, and to blame everyone and everything outside those small circles.

The challenges are huge, with no simple fixes, and for the moment, no solutions at all. There is no cure for the virus and no vaccine, and although we are impatient and antsy, we still need to keep our distance. The economic downturn will end eventually, but the recovery will be neither fast nor spread evenly, and only exacerbates existing income inequality and social divisions. Restoring justice and trust within our communities, providing hope for life, liberty, and the pursuit of happiness for all, is also not easy. Some of these problems have been with us for a long time, and others are more recent, but together they are formidable.

Our best course of action is to band together, pool our minds and our resources, try to understand different perspectives, and connect with people outside of our personal bubbles. Times will get better. The virus will die out, the economy will improve, and we will even make progress in curing our social and political troubles. How long will that take? No one can say, but our choices matter. We need to treat the virus seriously, find creative ways of making a living and helping others, and channel our frustrations productively.

What lessons can we learn, and what will we become? How will our response to this pandemic prepare us for future outbreaks? How can we structure our healthcare system and ensure that the burden of a future disease doesn't fall disproportionately on any segment of the population? How do we make our economy more resilient to shocks in the future? How do we address injustices in our society and heal the divisions between different subgroups?

We can succeed if we work together. The first step is to engage with others outside our small circles, to proactively seek out people who disagree with us with the purpose of understanding them. We need to open our minds to different ways of thinking and to empathize with people we don't like. To paraphrase Ian MacLaren - Let us be kind to each other, for most of us are fighting a tough battle. The problems we are facing are larger than one individual or any one group. Only by reaching out to others, with empathy and good will, will we emerge from these challenging times stronger and better prepared to meet the future.

Chapter 12

Hope, Fear and Opportunity

June 6

> *Life is statistical, and we don't control our fate, but if we make smart choices, we improve the odds that things will turn out okay.*

Nothing feels normal right now. Images of violence flood our screens, mayhem rules our streets, and we lurch from one trauma to the next. First the virus infected millions and killed hundreds of thousands. Then economic devastation brought financial insecurity and ruin. Now it's social unrest, fueled by generations of injustice and neglect, erupting into the public eye. Some of us might call for a return to normalcy, while others of us cry out for change, but we are united in our discomfort with the current situation, in which disease, economic hardship, and social distress have brought our world to a halt.

In these times, when the bottom drops out and the sky is falling, we are caught between our hopes and fears, our better and baser natures. It is tempting to give in to our fears and regain our sense of security by forcing a return to the old normal. Freedom might seem less important than security, and democracy less relevant than quiet in our streets. We might be attracted to leaders who promise us a return to a more tranquil past of health and prosperity, if we only give them the keys to the castle.

We might be tempted to pretend that the virus threat has passed, and resume our jobs and social lives. We might brush aside the violent suppression of peaceful protest and invite authoritarian rulers to impose law and order through arbitrary, prejudiced, and unfair means. But we can only support the imposition of draconian measures if we believe that we, personally, will not be their victim. History shows us that once we go down that path, things often don't end well, for all of us. Benjamin Franklin once said: "Those who would give up essential Liberty, to purchase a little temporary Safety, deserve neither Liberty nor Safety."

While we can't let our fears define us, nor can we ignore them. We need to encourage and support peaceful protest while condemning the looting of shops and the burning of buildings. We can't condone, tolerate, or excuse unacceptable behavior wherever it occurs. Even as we work for change, we need to understand and empathize with those among us who fear that the flame, once lit, might consume us all. We need to stop treating others as faceless enemies and realize that they are us. We have much in common, and our fates are intertwined.

The current situation creates an opening for productive dialogue and systemic change, but we can only capitalize on the opportunity if we don't let our fears divide us. It's been said that one shouldn't waste a good crisis, and this one is a potential goldmine. If we choose to let hope triumph over fear, we might reexamine our notion of normal and create a better future. We can imagine and strive for a stronger, more resilient and accessible health care system, a robust economy, and a safer, more equitable society. And then, with a combination of wise choices, collaboration, and luck, we might get there.

Chapter 13

Do Something, Anything

June 13

> *Feeling stuck? Bored? Anxious? Break your routine. Do something, anything, even one tiny step, and you might see a little ray of sunshine poke through the clouds.*

Some days we wake up feeling stuck in the mud. Weeks and months seem to run into each other, and things don't seem to be going much of anywhere. The pandemic still casts a pall over our lives, and while it ebbs and flows, will likely be with us for a while. The economy sputters along, occasionally showing signs of recovery only to be confronted with the reality that the road to prosperity will be long and bumpy and riven by setbacks. Indeed, the very fabric of our society seems to be threadbare, with deep structural challenges and partisan divisions pulling at the seams, and no magical solutions to pull us back together again. It's hard to feel hopeful.

Personally, the isolation we feel due to social distancing is starting to take a toll. It's been a long time. Although the virus is still spreading, and we know that caution is still warranted, we chafe against the rules and resent the restrictions. Financial insecurity is also spreading and deepening. While some have been in trouble for a while, others are now only starting to feel the anxiety and the pain, as furloughs turn into permanent layoffs, reserves start to run out, and the expenses keep coming. The news washes over us daily, from TV to social media, or in conversations with friends and family, flooding our consciousness with distress, anxiety, and fear. And it feels like tomorrow we will wake up to more of the same.

When the world around us seems to be falling apart, and it's hard to see the point in anything, we can either wallow in this feeling, sinking further into the quicksand, or try to move forward. It's hard to get things going and tempting to just coast along, hoping things get better without any effort from us. It takes energy to get the wheels moving again and pull the cart out of the mud, and we might not feel up to it. But we increase our chances of happiness by doing something, anything, to feel less stuck. We can start small, with baby steps, focusing on our local surroundings and finding tiny, almost effortless things we can do to try to kindle our hope.

What we choose to try might look different for each of us. It might involve tidying our home or fixing something that's been broken on our shelf, or creating a to-do list, or checking off one item as done. We could go for a walk or exercise, and we can soften the isolation by calling a friend or checking in on a neighbor. As we take our first step and then our second and beyond, we should note what we've accomplished, and over time, take heart from our trail of small successes.

Chapter 14

Summer is Here!

June 20

> *If we can find something to be grateful for in the midst of crisis and disaster, we are forever blessed.*

Suddenly, summer is upon us! With the solstice hours away, we revel in hours of daylight and bask under the scorching sun. Some of us enjoy the caressing warmth of the sun, while others wilt from the oppressive heat. Some of us run outside to savor the moment, while others of us hide in airconditioned rooms, waiting for autumn. But love it or hate it, summer is here, reminding us again of our small place in the universe.

We can't will summer away by labeling it a hoax or fake news, nor can we make it linger by declaring our loyalty or love. Summer doesn't care what we believe or want. It simply is what it is, coming and going every year. We can pretend it hasn't really arrived, but summer doesn't mind. The sun will still burn our skin, and the heat will make us sweat just the same. We can get angry, or dance with joy, but either way, the sun will rise tomorrow. Summer isn't good or bad—it's just summer. We'd like to control it, but that is not within our grasp, and the sooner we realize that and stop fighting it, the happier we will be.

But accepting summer doesn't have to mean living in misery. While we do not control the weather, we can and should be masters of our experience. We are in charge of our decisions, our narratives, and our reactions, and it is those things, more than the weather, that determine the quality of our lives. It is our choice to wear a hat and sunscreen for protection, or to wake up with the birds to enjoy the early morning breezes. It is our choice to stay hydrated and to seek shade in the midday sun, or if possible, find a cool body of water or airconditioned space to restore our spirits. We make decisions every moment, and those decisions have consequences.

In addition, we narrate stories that profoundly impact our experience. We might frame ourselves as victims of summer or look for opportunities to have fun. We can count the days till autumn, or we can embrace the long days and warmth. We can tell ourselves that summer is to be endured or be enjoyed, and whatever we tell ourselves, our experiences will follow. Finally, we can manage our emotional reactions. If the heat makes us crabby, we shouldn't take it out on those around us. If we feel elated by the sun's rays, we should still find empathy in our hearts for those who suffer from its heat.

Summer is here, and so is the pandemic, the faltering economy, and our conflicted society. To increase happiness and minimize misery, we must try to accept our world as it is while managing our stories, reactions, and choices.

Chapter 15

Information, Beliefs, and Conclusions

June 28

> *"Facts do not cease to exist because they are ignored"*
> *—Aldous Huxley.*

Too often we cling to our beliefs, even when they are contradicted by the data. In the end, reality wins - we get hurt falling down the stairs even if we don't believe in gravity. It's hard to know what to believe any more. Is the pandemic ahead of us, behind us, or all around us? Should we worry more about people who sicken and die from the virus or those who are going hungry from the financial fallout of the lockdowns? Is it worse to leave the house and risk getting sick or to continue isolation and suffer from loneliness, anxiety, and depression? Every opinion and course of action has its advocates and adherents, and it's getting increasingly difficult to distinguish the signal from the noise.

In trying to understand what's going on and deciding what to do, we let our opinions bias us. A recent survey showed that 65% of Republicans feel comfortable going into a restaurant now while only 28% of Democrats do. How is this possible? Are they physiologically distinct? Aren't they neighbors? Don't they both have access to the same internet or news? Somehow, similar people come to divergent conclusions regarding what's going on and how to respond.

The Ladder of Inference, proposed by Chris Argyris in 1970 and published by Peter Senge in The Fifth Discipline, explains why. According to this model, we all experience and observe our surroundings, but we don't see the same things. Each of us is only exposed to a subset of observations, which we then filter by only looking in certain directions and noticing different information. We live in different areas, look at different news sources, and remember different things. We then interpret our observations through our cultural lenses and personal experiences, creating narratives and coming to different conclusions from each other. We develop theories and adopt beliefs to guide our behavior, and take actions consistent with those beliefs, which then feed back into our next set of observations, and the whole cycle reinforces itself.

To make better decisions, we need to question every step in this process. We need to move beyond our silos and echo chambers and to seek out the facts for ourselves. How did we select our data and in what ways have we limited or biased our information? What assumptions have we made and what meaning have we attached to our experiences? We need to push back on our conclusions, challenge our beliefs, and examine our actions.

It's time to call bull***t, not just on our adversaries, but on ourselves. When our eye is drawn to a meme that confirms what we already think, when our leader says something we want to believe, and especially before we act, we need to ask for proof. "Show me! Prove it! Give me the data!" And then we need to examine our sources and question their credibility. Where did they get their data? How scientific and reliable are their methods? Lastly, we need to reach out to others, especially those who disagree with us, not to refute their arguments, but to enrich our understanding, calibrate our own conclusions, and move forward together.

Chapter 16

Setbacks Happen

July 6

> *Hang in there! Sometimes that's the best we can do in the moment, and often, even hanging in there is a struggle. But the moment will pass, and a new day will dawn. Prepare for the worst, hope for the best, stay optimistic, and never give up.*

In business, sports, politics, and our personal lives, there are winning streaks and losses, good days and bad. There are times when things go well for us, and we feel like invincible heroes, and other times when the ground opens up at our feet and threatens to swallow us whole. Setbacks happen, and sometimes really big ones that knock the breath right out of us and cause us to question who we are, what we are made of, and what we are capable of accomplishing. Significant setbacks can increase our self-doubt and damage our self-confidence.

And yet setbacks are expected and inevitable. Life is full of disappointments - in ourselves, other people, our accomplishments, and our circumstances. Everything we do requires both sound decision-making and luck, and at any given moment, either one might be lacking. Sometimes we make poor decisions because we are missing critical information, are distracted, follow false logic, or are emotionally needy. Sometimes we make reasoned, well thought-out decisions, do everything right, but things go wrong anyway. We are not perfect, and the world around us isn't fair.

We often react poorly to setbacks. We might ignore them, pretending that things are better than they are and that the bad thing didn't just happen. Unfortunately, denial, while comfortable, can be dangerous. Unaware of what's going on, we can't respond productively. Sometimes, especially if we were careful but things went wrong anyway, we look for someone else to blame, lashing out at scapegoats in our helplessness and anger. Alternatively, we might look inward, blaming and castigating ourselves and using the setback to generate a negative self-narrative. None of these responses are particularly helpful.

Instead, it is best to accept the idea that setbacks happen sometimes, and when they do, to manage our responses, learn valuable lessons, and move on without yielding to the temptation to beat on ourselves or on others. The first impact of a setback is almost always emotional. We might feel shocked, overwhelmed, sad, angry, or frustrated. That initial emotional impulse is powerful and can activate our fight or flight instincts, making it difficult for us to respond productively. To regain our composure, we need to slow down, recognize our emotions for what they are, and give ourselves time to recover.

We then need to analyze matters to distinguish the facts from our perceptions and assumptions, or the stories we've created around them. We also need to derive lessons and make new plans, so we can recover and move on. We must focus on the present and the future rather than the recent past. What's done is done. Then we need to act, taking steps to transform ourselves and our future. Setbacks happen. We can't control or stop them, but we can prevent them from defining us or our experience. By accepting reality, managing our responses, embracing life's lessons, and taking actions, we can emerge happier, stronger, and more resilient.

Chapter 17

Life is Good

July 11

> *Gratitude, luck, and optimism are intimately linked. Looking for positives gives us the courage to hope for lucky outcomes, and being grateful for our good fortune encourages us to stay optimistic. Start with any of the three, and the others might follow in a self-perpetuating cycle of joy.*

Life is how we look at it, and the more we slow down, look around us, savor the little things, focus on the positives, and appreciate everything we have, the better our experience. Of course, there are tough times, and not everything we encounter is so wonderful. Some things in our lives are downright awful, difficult, and traumatic. But even within difficult times, we can find opportunities to notice the little bright spots.

Some of us are naturally optimistic and enjoy our day-to-day, but for others of us, the skies are normally cloudier, and learning to see the world in a positive light requires a change of focus. Learning to celebrate our lives involves a great deal of effort and persistence, but if we succeed, the payoff is huge. No matter what life throws at us, what challenges and obstacles we encounter, and what miseries we suffer, our experience will still be joyful.

We first need to slow down, since we often pack on too

many obligations, activities, and deadlines. We rush from task to task and from checklist to checklist, often without asking if what we are doing is meaningful to us or useful to others. Having talked ourselves into a frenzy and conditioned ourselves to cascade from one activity to the next, we feel burdened, stressed, and anxious, and can't really enjoy the journey. We need to stop, slow down, and realize that the Earth rotated about its axis before we were born and will continue to do so after we are gone. We're not that important, and neither are the items on our checklist.

Then we need to look around. To paraphrase Yogi Berra - You can observe a lot by looking. Once we slow down, we can start noticing the trees and flowers, the cool breeze rustling through the leaves, the clouds whisking across the sky, the brilliance of the full moon, the stars sparkling at night, the laughter of a child, or the sight of two friends walking side by side. We can marvel at the sight of an airplane overhead or learn to distinguish the unique chirping of the birds, and even learn to appreciate moments of utter silence.

Savoring these little things and recognizing how lucky we are to have them is what makes life so preciously wonderful. Even if we find the people we live with to be annoying, we do ourselves a favor by focusing on their positive qualities and enjoying the little moments with them. Even if we hate our jobs, we can often find some aspects of the work that are more enjoyable and fulfilling. Then, we should be grateful for all of these little things and for our ability to notice and enjoy them. Shakespeare wrote that "nothing is good or bad but thinking makes it so." Life can be challenging and hard. That's not up to us. But life is also good, if only we choose to make it so.

Chapter 18

Negotiating in a Pandemic

July 18

> *Negotiation is at its core an emotional process. Of course, strategies, skills, and tactics all matter, but in the end, our effectiveness depends upon our ability to manage our own emotions and influence the emotional responses of others.*

Negotiations can be nerve-racking, even under normal circumstances. We want what we want but are afraid that things will go terribly wrong, and we'll end up worse off than before. Conflict and uncertainty are hard, and we feel unmatched by the other party's power, knowledge, or skill. We don't know where to begin, or whether we should even bother, and the very idea fills us with doubt.

How long should we chitchat? How do we ask for what we want? How far can we push without damaging the relationship? What concessions should we make, and where do we hold firm? How do we respond to the other person's offers? Is there something we are missing? Is the other person really going to carry out their commitments, or will we be left with little to show for our efforts?

The pandemic makes these issues more challenging. We always negotiate in light of our alternatives, and for many of us, the alternatives have gotten scarier. Negotiating a job offer is tougher if we've been out of work for several months and have no other offers to fall back on. Asking for a promotion at work feels risky in light of recent furloughs and layoffs. If we are trying to sell our house and expect the market to go down, we might feel desperate to make concessions to a buyer, imagining that no other buyers will come along.

In addition to questioning our alternatives, there is also a more pervasive, pandemic-related anxiety hanging over many people these days. We worry that we or someone in our care might get sick, or that the economy might crumble under a second lockdown, or that our money might run out. Seeking safety, we look for the comfort of certainty and shy away from the inherent unpredictability of negotiations. But at the same time, without negotiating, we limit our outcomes and minimize our opportunities.

Negotiating during a pandemic involves engaging with the process under stressful and anxiety-provoking conditions. To do so effectively, we need to focus inward first. We need to notice when we feel stressed, identify what is making us feel this way, and understand the impact of the stress on us as negotiators. We need to prepare more extensively before we start to negotiate, and to slow down the process when our reactions become counter-productive.

Despite the fear, we still need to ask for more and then listen carefully to the response. We need to ask questions, respecting the other person's interests but also articulating our own. Finally, while our alternatives may not be as favorable as they were before, we still need to be ready to go to them if the need arises. So, negotiating in a pandemic, while more challenging, can still be effective for us, so long as we prepare beforehand, manage our emotions in real time, assert our interests carefully, and listen more than we talk.

Chapter 19

Victory Lap

July 27

> *No matter how fast or hard we work and how many boxes we check, there are always more boxes and always more tasks. If we slow down and focus on the blank spaces between the boxes, we might find meaning in the emptiness and learn to enjoy in the journey.*

In our drive to accomplish enough, we might not notice when we've achieved something remarkable and simply move on to the next item on our list. Our lists are lengthy, and our days are short, so we constantly feel overloaded. Aiming high is fine, but it's also important to know when to slow down, stop, and savor a moment. Merely moving on from one task to the next diminishes our experience and devalues our accomplishments. We benefit from pausing the race to take a victory lap, smile, and enjoy a feeling of satisfaction at what we've done.

If doing so is difficult for us, it might help us to try and figure out why. Why do we move on without pause, forever on the treadmill? Perhaps we have our reasons – financial security, demands from others, or a need to affirm our own self-worth through accomplishments. But we might also recognize that we have a choice in how to frame things, and that it might help us lead more satisfied lives if we can balance our drive to achieve with our desire to savor moments.

Celebrating small wins can actually help us achieve greater things. By breaking large problems into smaller ones, we can solve the pieces one at a time on the way to the complete solution. While our schedule might force us to transition quickly from one problem to the next, we can still take a moment, breathe, and recognize that completing the previous task is an accomplishment worth noting. We can pat ourselves on the back, reward ourselves in some way, or point out what we've done to someone else and get some external affirmation of our success.

At the same time, we shouldn't confuse taking a victory lap with declaring victory. After all, our momentary respite does not make the rest of the list go away. In celebrating our success, we must not get complacent, or think we're done and that the problem is solved. No matter what we've accomplished, or how many accolades we've received, there are always more challenges to overcome and more lives to impact. Whether in war, medicine, business, or elsewhere, declaring victory too quickly can bring dire consequences.

We are at our best when we are humble and modest, appreciating ourselves and the moment while keeping things in perspective. Sir Isaac Newton was quoted as saying, "I do not know what I may appear to the world, but to myself I seem to have been only like a boy playing on the sea-shore, and diverting myself in now and then finding a smoother pebble or a prettier shell than ordinary, whilst the great ocean of truth lay all undiscovered before me." Newton's modesty reminds us to be humble and realize that our job is not yet done. But every now and then, we should still let ourselves get excited, pause, and take victory lap.

Chapter 20

If We Don't Ask

August 2

> *The first negotiation is always with yourself - knowing what you want, having the courage to ask for it, getting over your anxieties, preparing ahead of time, developing your skills, and managing your emotions.*

Rejection is frightening, especially in times of crisis. When we get turned away, it can disappoint us, hurt our feelings, and lower our confidence. When we hear "no," we might start to question ourselves. Was our request unreasonable? Did we offend? Is there something we didn't know or should have considered? We imagine answers to these questions and associate the act of asking with personal rejection and hurt. Especially now, we might focus on the risks and dangers and might hold back in asking for what we need.

But if we don't ask, we don't get. If we don't ask for a discount from a vendor, we are unlikely to get one. If we don't ask our customers to close sales, they might delay their purchases or might never buy at all. If we don't ask for that upgrade, favor, or work assignment, and instead hope that it will come to us on its own, we risk fairly long odds. Too often we toil at our desks, produce great work, and put in long hours, hoping that our manager notices our strong effort and rewards us with a raise, a promotion or a bonus, but find that we get overlooked. Instead, the promotion, nice office, or financial reward goes to our colleague, who may not have made the effort, but asked for the recognition.

Life's not fair. In a perfect world, we would get what we deserve without having to ask for it. In a better world, defined by collaboration and generosity, the people around us would be looking for ways to help us out and to reward us for our accomplishments, just as we would be doing the same for them. But in our current reality, we must learn to ask for what we need. It takes energy to overcome our reluctance to ask. Before each request, we have to build ourselves up, rehearse what we are going to say, and steel ourselves to withstand the rejection.

But much of this mental anguish is unnecessary. The way to overcome our fear of asking is to start doing it, as often as we can and wherever the opportunities arise. We can ask for little things, such as a refill of our coffee or help in moving a bookcase, and slowly build up to more significant requests, such as a new laptop or a funding for our project. As we start asking, we will certainly get some rejections, but people will also say "yes" far more often than we expect. We will soon realize that we've been leaving a lot of value on the table by not asking, that our requests are a much bigger deal for us than they are for the other person, and that hearing "no" as an answer isn't all that terrible. Over time, we can lose our fear of asking and become better at meeting our needs.

Chapter 21

Fear of Conflict

August 9

> *If we minimize risk and take the safest path, we also minimize opportunity. Adventure awaits, and sometimes the danger of the journey is less than the danger of withering by the hearth.*

Some people seek out conflict, but most of us tend to avoid it. We find conflict uncomfortable and get panicky when forced to confront someone. We postpone important conversations, avoid controversial topics, pretend that we're okay with things when we're not, and stop ourselves from negotiating to meet our own needs. While conflict is part of life and can often lead to positive outcomes in the form of breakthroughs and new ideas, many of us feel endangered by it.

In Crucial Conversations: Tools for Talking When Stakes Are High, Al Switzler, Joseph Grenny, and Ron McMillan postulate that constructive dialog is impossible if people feel unsafe. In Difficult Conversations: How to Discuss What Matters Most, Douglas Stone, Bruce Patton, and Sheila Heen note that we often experience disagreement negatively on the emotional level. But what is it that makes conflict so scary? In Collywobbles: How to Negotiate When Negotiating Makes You Nervous, I add a different approach, looking at conflict as a stress factor that amplifies our fears.

Conflict is scary on multiple levels. First, there is the fear of tangible hurt. We might negotiate poorly and get less than we had hoped or end up worse off than we started. In trying to bargain for better terms, we might end up losing the customer. The second is fear of relationship damage. We are sensitive to how others respond to us. We want to confront our neighbor about the barking dog but are afraid of adversely impacting our relationship. The third fear involves emotional pain. Negotiating can make us feel badly about ourselves. We remember the sting of getting rejected when we asked our boss for a promotion, and we don't want to experience that again.

Conflict amplifies these concerns. When we confront someone, there is a chance that we might suffer damage in tangible, relational, or emotional ways. Since engaging in conflict requires some initiative, the added emotional energy to get past our fears and take action is often more than we can muster. Instead, we forgo opportunities, settle for less, suffer indignities, and fail to follow the advice we would give others. We tell ourselves stories and make up excuses why letting things go is better than asserting our needs, and we retreat.

To overcome our fear of conflict, we need first to understand it. We need to determine which of the three fears are driving our behavior and why we perceive the conflict as dangerous. We need to prepare ourselves on the tangible and emotional levels so we can assess dangers realistically and put our fears in perspective. We need to slow down and manage our emotions in real time and to reach out to others for help when we can't overcome our fears on our own. By doing these things, the fear of conflict, while present, will no longer define our interactions, and we can become better self-advocates.

Chapter 22

Once Upon a Time

August 16

> *If you find yourself mired in negative thoughts, self-doubt, or anxiety, pause and ask yourself, "what am I telling myself right now?" You create your own reality.*

We are a storytelling species. In Sapiens: A Brief History of Humankind, Yuval Harari attempts to explain how a relatively insignificant ape, wandering around in small family groups on the savannahs of Africa seventy thousand years ago, came to dominate the planet. He asserts that our success owes to our ability to invent fictions and believe in them collectively. Nations, corporations, money, and other cultural connections that bind us to each other allow us to collaborate flexibly and in large numbers. Individually, we are still relatively small, weak, insignificant apes, but collectively, we have become a dominant force on the planet.

In addition to the stories we invent to guide our interactions, we also create and then live within stories that exist solely in our own minds and aren't shared with other people, sometimes even those closest to us. We each have a creation myth, recounting our journey from birth to adulthood, placing us within a family, culture, religion, nation or country, and explaining where we fit within the world around us. Initially, we were given a story by our family members and society, but over time, we adopted and evolved this story as our own.

Ultimately, we become our stories and in turn, our stories define our life experience. We repeat narratives in our minds, cementing how we think about ourselves and everything we encounter. We filter new data and experiences through our stories, assimilating those that reinforce our beliefs while rejecting and forgetting those that contradict what we imagine to be true. We seek out people who agree with us, read and follow sources that confirm what we think, and are increasingly challenged to distinguish fact from fiction.

But not all of these stories serve us well. We can repeat very negative stories about ourselves. We psyche ourselves out of pursuing opportunities by telling ourselves that we are not good enough. We judge ourselves harshly and get angry with ourselves. We describe our world as dangerous and become anxious, looking around corners for threats and imagining bad-intentioned foes coming to harm us. We worry constantly about what could or might be happening soon and lose sight of what is right in front of our noses. So many of us experience misery and fear, much of which is driven by the narratives in our minds.

If we can recognize and hear what we are telling ourselves, we can regain control of our experiences and become happier. Our stories exist solely in our minds, and we can therefore learn to manage them. We can try to be conscious authors of our stories rather than their victims, and to reshape our stories to more accurately reflect the reality around us and frame things in a positive direction. Once upon a time, we were given a story; it's time we own it and strive to reshape our lives for the better.

Chapter 23

Deal or No Deal?

August 25

> *If you try to accommodate every request, you end up overcommitting and underperforming. You try to make everyone happy but end up making no one happy, especially yourself. Learn how to say "no" to some things in order to deliver on the most important priorities.*

Walking away from an opportunity in the middle of a pandemic can be terrifying, but sometimes the best deal is no deal at all. In every negotiation, if we don't come to an agreement with the other party, we will try to meet our interests in other ways. Unfortunately, we often want to come to an agreement so badly—especially after investing a great deal of time and effort—that we keep trying even when it's pretty obvious that calling it off is the smart thing to do.

Our ability and willingness to walk away depends on what we perceive might happen. If we are negotiating terms with one vendor and have another vendor lined up, then walking away might be fairly doable. But what if the consequence means delaying our product launch? Then it's much harder, and we might continue negotiating even when it no longer makes sense, or even if we find out that the vendor has been overcharging us and treating us poorly.

Walking away is scary. We might be afraid of financial loss, of damaging relationships, or of emotional distress, and since all of those might happen if the negotiation fails, we can become panicky and give away value just to close the deal. In addition, as we negotiate, we become involved with the other party, and walking away feels like we're letting them down. Knowing this, they might do everything in their power to impact our perception of the risks and rewards in order to coerce us into an agreement.

If we are so committed to this negotiation that we can't get ourselves to walk away, we become needy and give the other party power over us. They can keep making demands and pushing us to our limit, and though unhappy, we will keep backing down, feeling like we have no choice. But we always have a choice, and although walking away comes with risks and costs, sometimes it's the best thing to do. Maybe there is no profitable deal to be had. Maybe we come to realize that this person is not someone we want to do business with. Maybe our alternatives aren't just survivable, but actually better for us.

So, before we start negotiating, we need to think of alternatives to pursue if there is no agreement. We should research the costs and consequences of each and then imagine that we have to go to them. The longer we think about them, the less scary they might become. By preparing our alternatives in advance and incorporating them into our strategy, we become stronger negotiators, willing to end the negotiation if we can't meet our interests with the other party. If the best deal is no deal at all, we will be ready to walk away.

Chapter 24

Get Lost!

August 29

> *Sometimes the best, wisest, most productive course of action is to lie down in a hammock and take a nap. "Don't underestimate the value of doing nothing, of just going along, listening to all the things you can't hear, and not bothering." —Winnie the Pooh*

We generally don't like feeling lost, unsure of where we are, and unclear as to the path forward. Feeling directionless can be uncomfortable, and we seek structure and instructions to help us orient ourselves and point out where we need to go. We want to wake up at home, or at least know how to get back there. We want to know our purpose and plan for the day, and what success looks like. We want someone to tell us the rules and give us a schedule. We find comfort in our routines.

But getting lost can be very healthy. When we are lost, if we can let go of our anxiety, we can start to truly experience where we are. We slow down, get curious, and observe the amazing things, large and small, around us. Allowing ourselves to enjoy feeling lost involves a leap of faith – the belief that sometime in the future, by some means, we will no longer be lost, and will be okay. If we take that leap, manage our panic, and open our eyes, then we can embark on a journey of discovery and wonder.

We can take the chance and literally step off the beaten path, purposely choosing unfamiliar routes, wandering into unknown neighborhoods, and exploring new places. Turning off our GPS, we can focus less on where we are going and more on what we can discover. As we meander, we might detour into charming alleyways and stumble onto hidden gardens, finding secret gems that only the locals know. We can engage strangers in conversation, get a window into their world and, on the way, meet ourselves.

Sometimes we are better off without a schedule, living in the moment, allowing ourselves the luxury of boredom. We can turn off our devices, quiet our minds, and compartmentalize our obligations, to-do lists, and goals. There is value in letting ourselves float in time once in a while, letting our brains idle, and focusing on the here and now. Recent studies (see the January 4, 2019 issue of Time Magazine for example), have indicated that boredom can spur our creativity and improve our mental health.

That is when we can daydream and get lost in thought. When our minds wander, we think of new ideas and invent novel solutions to unsolved problems. We imagine new possibilities, see things from different perspectives, and express our creativity in extraordinary ways. Not knowing the answers, we ask more interesting questions, and make remarkable discoveries.

In the past, we routinely found ourselves lost or bored. Now, with cellphones, GPS, and social media, we have to make a conscious choice if we want to give ourselves the gift of feeling lost. We are a powerful species, and our success comes partly from knowing where we are, where we are going, and what to do next. But once in a while, we should get lost, let go, and discover a very different definition of success.

Chapter 25

What is in the Way?

September 5

> *There is often a gap between how things are and how we'd like them to be, and that space can get filled with frustration, anger, and despair. By replacing frustration with acceptance, anger with optimism, and despair with determination, we achieve better outcomes and have a much better time in the process.*

Oftentimes we know what we would like to do, but the challenge is in getting ourselves to do it. Whether we are looking to negotiate, diet, exercise, do our jobs, or make decisions, the problem isn't that we don't know, but that something else gets in the way. We make plans, prepare, develop skills, and then somehow, between the planning and the execution, things go wrong. We want to lose weight, but that brownie just looks too good. We want to get our work done, but we're just so tired. We want to negotiate for more but get overwhelmed and can't get ourselves to ask.

We find ourselves trapped in a cycle of knowing but not doing and falling short of our goals. How then can we get beyond the hopes, dreams, and plans, and start accomplishing the things we would like to achieve. The social scientist, Kurt Lewin, described a model for behavior change that he called Force Field Analysis. Lewin's premise was that every situation is held in place by balance of forces, some of which promote the behavior we want and others that resist it. Force Field Analysis helps explain why things are the way they are and provides ideas as to how to move forward.

For example, we might feel unfulfilled in our careers and want to switch fields, but as the weeks turn into months and years, are still stuck in our old jobs. Why haven't we made a move? We know we want to! Some of the forces that would help us switch might include job satisfaction, career advancement, better pay, day-to-day happiness, and a desire to do something new. On the other hand, there are other forces getting in the way of making a change. We might be afraid of starting over, unconfident in learning new skills, risk averse, comfortable in our commute, or waiting for stock options to vest. The balance of these forces keeps us right where we are – dreaming about change but stuck in our jobs indefinitely.

The way to change our results is by either increasing the promoting forces or by weakening the resisting ones. We can increase the pressure on ourselves to make a change by asking our family members to nag us, buying a new house to create financial distress, or doing such a bad job at work that our boss might fire us. But increasing these promoting forces requires a great deal of energy on our part and creates new resisting forces. Instead, we should focus on weakening the forces that are in the way. If we are worried about skills, we can take classes. If we are risk averse, we can get a home equity loan to create a financial cushion for ourselves. We deserve to meet our goals, and by removing the barriers blocking our path, we can achieve them more effectively.

Chapter 26

Life is Short

September 12

> *If we don't make time for the truly important things in our life, we won't realize until it's too late that they have passed us by.*

Life is short, and we are soon forgotten. Our days seem long, but the years go by quickly, and over time, the energy and vigor of our youth give way to fatigue and frailty. Whoever we are, wherever in the world, no matter our age or station in life, today is the youngest we are going to be. This is not depressing or morbid, but simply fact. Today is our day, and the only direction is forward. The choice we have is what to do with it.

If we are to seize the day and avoid looking back with regret, we must use our time wisely. Every day overwhelms us with tasks and to-do lists, and at the end of too many days, we look back and feel hollow, like all we did was run in place, never accomplishing anything meaningful. We need to give careful thought to our values and to understand what gives us satisfaction and meaning. Then we need to allocate some time to focus on these valuable activities, even if it means putting off some nagging, urgent tasks. In the words of Stephen Covey, "First Things First."

When we are gone, all that remains is what we've left behind – the things we created, the people we touched, the shared memory of our community. As we live our lives, we write our story, and then others pick up on that story to absorb it into their own. David Eagleman said that "There are three deaths. The first is when the body ceases to function. The second is when the body is consigned to the grave. The third is that moment, sometime in the future, when our name is spoken for the last time." If we are kind to others, build communities, and leave a legacy, our stories will endure.

But finding meaning doesn't consign us to a life of drudgery. We must balance our long-term goals with the short-term objective of living our lives. We can and should have fun along the way, and absolutely shouldn't take ourselves too seriously. We must look for joy and find pleasure in the little things, our interactions with others and the activities we pursue. We improve our experience by paying attention to the small details around us, from the rustle of the leaves, to the laughter of a child, the satisfaction of a job well done, or a chance conversation.

With the passage of time, we become richer in memories and gain new perspectives. The things we do and see today become our cherished memories tomorrow, so we should strive to do things that are memorable. We also gain by pausing to reflect on everything we do and come across in order to enrich our perspectives. Life is short and sometimes hard, but it can also be beautiful and wonderful, if we are mindful and make it so.

Chapter 27

Bad Things Happen

September 21

> *Sometimes it's better not to plan, and instead to just float along like a leaf in a stream, bobbing up and down in the water, getting snagged on the occasional rock, and letting the future surprise us.*

Sometimes bad things happen. The bad guys win, and despite our planning and hard work, our hopes get dashed, our dreams shattered. Life is very hard sometimes; and yet, it goes on, days leading into weeks, then months and years, as generations go by. The world has always produced a mix of good and bad outcomes, and likely always will, but that is little consolation when staring disappointment in the face. How can we deal with the notion that sometimes life feels neither fair nor kind, and we feel crushed by events?

Breathe!

As long as we can still breathe in and out, even with difficulty, as long as we have thoughts, no matter how miserable, as long as we can still feel, even if we need to cry or scream, we are still here, and have survived to fight another day. Let there be no illusions! This likely isn't our last disappointment, or the worst that we'll endure, and we might not see the way forward. It's foolish to think that things can't get worse. They can, and we might be in for greater difficulty ahead, but although down, we are not totally out, and for the moment, that's the best we can do.

Next, we need to slow down, focus local and small, and try to find something, anything we can do. When things go wrong we need to give ourselves some time to cope and regroup. Rushing into action can sometimes work but often creates new problems. We should let ourselves grieve our loss, respect our disappointment and pain, and take some time to process. But we can also start healing ourselves by doing what we can, the small deeds that are within our capacity to influence. Wallowing in misery and inaction too long isn't healthy either.

Despite the difficulty, we need to try to keep looking for the possibilities. It's hard to stay optimistic when all hope feels lost, and yet life is statistical – along with all the bad, there will eventually be some good, and when it comes, we need to be ready for it. If, after the initial shock, we can refocus our attention on the positives, we can start noticing some good things happening, even if they are small, and over time, grow them into a new reality.

Finally, we can seek out others for companionship and support. It's unhealthy to worry alone – we lose perspective, and our thoughts can go from bad to worse. In addition, by connecting with others, we might find ways of shifting focus away from ourselves and into helping others with their challenges. There is no shortage of misery, and we can make a difference. Bad things do happen, but that's not the end of the story, only the current chapter. The rest is up to us.

Chapter 28

Feeling Powerless

September 26

> *Before a negotiation, it can help if we are little bit nervous, so long as we translate this nervousness into extra preparation. It's better to be over-prepared and pleasantly surprised than over-confident and blindsided.*

Nothing makes us feel more powerless than being locked in our homes due to a global pandemic, but that makes it difficult for us to negotiate for our needs. In other times, when we feel more powerful, we might negotiate more forcefully and try to get lower prices, higher salaries, or greater value. We approach our negotiations with confidence, make bold demands, and take advantage of our relative strength.

But what about different times, like now, when we are the desperate ones, when we are looking for a job in a bad economy, staring unemployment in the face? How do we negotiate when our company is about to run out of money and the investors are circling for the kill? How can we still be effective negotiators when facing overwhelming odds and feeling powerless?

Life is a game of probabilities, and sometimes our odds aren't great, but we still have to take the cards we've been dealt and do the best we can with them. In order to do anything, we first need to overcome our sense of helplessness. If we are overwhelmed by feeling powerless, we will be ineffective unless we recognize and manage our emotional responses. If we name what we're feeling, give ourselves some time to recover, and develop strategies to keep the panic at bay, we can start thinking again and assess our options.

We must have some power, since the other party is still negotiating with us. They must need something, or they wouldn't bother. To figure out what that is, we need to broaden our notion of power. They might have positional authority as our boss, or financial power as our customer, or resource power as our investor, but they must be missing something and have determined that the best way to get it is to talk to us. Our power might come from our knowledge, skills, talents, relationships, reputation, or patience. Alternatively, their vulnerability might derive from internal issues that are hidden from our sight yet drive their behavior.

To find and cultivate our power, we need to be patient and persistent. We must ask probing questions, listen closely to the answers that come back, and use silence to prompt them to reveal more information. We must cultivate allies and create alternative choices for ourselves to make us less dependent on this negotiation, and we should stay optimistic that favorable options will develop through the conversation.

Sometimes their power might be overwhelming, and we might be forced to accept unfavorable terms, but even then, it's not over. The game continues, and there will be other negotiations in our path. We should use the experience to learn for the next time around, to hone our skills and build up our strengths. Power is part circumstance and part attitude, so we should do the best with what we have and then prepare better strategies for future negotiations.

Chapter 29

Out of Our Minds

October 3

> *We need to spend more time out in nature to help us regain our center and sense of perspective. Even if our only access to nature is a city park, sidewalk, balcony, or view out the window, we can connect with a patch of grass, a squirrel on a branch, or a wisp of cloud in the sky and remember that we are just small pieces in a greater whole.*

When someone tells us that we are out of our minds, we often take this as an insult, implying that we are unreasonable, irrational, or insane. But maybe it's not all bad, since these days the greater danger might be to remain locked within our own minds. As our society becomes more polarized, as we find ourselves more isolated, as we spend more time judging than perceiving, we run the risk of becoming trapped, unable to escape our own narratives.

We are unable to perceive the world around us for what it is. We filter our observations through limited, distorting perceptions and see only what we want to see or already believe. If our world is a dark and negative place, our thoughts get darker with time and our negativity increases. Increasingly disconnected from reality, we battle illusions, fail to heed true signs of danger, and make suboptimal decisions. Only if we are freed from the shackles of our thoughts and interpretations can we begin to perceive and then examine the world around us more objectively, and in turn, make wiser choices.

When we open our minds, we also become empathetic, striving to understand people's concerns rather than rushing to judgment about them. We can focus on listening, hearing different perspectives, considering alternative points of view, and exploring different solutions. Getting out of our own minds allows us to connect to other people and build communities, not just within our small circle of like-minded believers, but also across boundaries. Alternatively, when we stay locked within our minds, we go in circles, reinforcing whatever thoughts are already there while isolating ourselves from others.

The notion of being out of our minds can be terrifying, implying a debilitating loss of control. While it may be unwise to simply "let it all hang out" and dismantle all of our filters, there is also a danger in self-managing to the extreme. We exert control by one part of our mind to suppress other parts of ourselves, and the illusion of control becomes a proxy for living in fear. We worry too much about control, fearing that if we just let ourselves be, and allow the world to see an unvarnished version of ourselves, we would be shunned. We secretly believe that if other people knew us as we know ourselves, they wouldn't like us. It is sad to live in fear and exhilarating to feel with abandon.

Our minds are what make us uniquely human. While cherishing our unique capabilities, we should also remember that like any tool, our thoughts can serve our interests or undermine them. The more aware we are of our own motivations, fears, and judgments— the filters that distort our perceptions—the more we can optimize the balance between using our minds and allowing ourselves, to once in a while, to abandon control.

Chapter 30

Overwhelmed

October 11

> *When I feel stressed and busy because I've got too many important things that I need to do, it helps me to remember that (1) some of those things I do by choice and can drop, (2) some I might be able to postpone, and (3) very few things in life are all that important. Then I might still be busy, but perhaps a bit less stressed.*

Life has become overwhelming for many of us, faced with new challenges, not knowing exactly who or what to believe, and burdened by worry and fear. We are largely creatures of habit, but now our old habits no longer apply. We used to work in an office, but now we work from home. We used to get our hair cut professionally, but now we let our family members cut it or let it grow out. Some of us traveled frequently, but now haven't seen the inside of an airplane in months.

Yet, life goes on. We need to put food on the table, educate our children, take care of those around us, and find joy and meaning in our new routines. It's all very difficult to get used to. Getting out of bed is tougher. We used to go to the gym, but now work out in the yard or often, not at all. Remember stopping for that latte before work? No driving, no office, homemade coffee. Do we put on real clothes, comb our hair, or clean off our desk? Maybe, but it's such a bother.

And as we get past eating breakfast, brushing our teeth, and sitting down to work, around us, the house begins to awaken. Various family members emerge from slumber, stagger into showers, and walk around like zombies, just as overwhelmed with their day as we are with ours. Our children click into their classrooms, try to stay engaged, and eat up our bandwidth. Like our internet connection, our thoughts become slower and choppier with every interruption. We know that we are overwhelmed when the things that would normally come easily to us now require concentration and effort. They just feel difficult.

We go from virtual meeting to virtual meeting, sharing documents, making small talk, and trying to connect with our colleagues. Somehow, this feels more exhausting than regular meetings, especially when the meetings just run into one another in never ending video calls. And at the end of the day, do we know when and how to stop working and start living our lives? Can we somehow separate our home life from the work we do all day? Can we disconnect and relax, or devote the proper attention to our loved ones?

So, many of us are in a daze and act overwhelmed even if we are not aware of it. If we can notice what we are feeling and the impact on our behavior, we can get through this. It's okay to be overwhelmed now. It's appropriate, given everything that's going on. But we won't stay this way forever. Things will change again, some of the things we loved will return, and we will discover new opportunities. To get through this time, we can connect with others, share coping strategies, and remember that we are not alone in feeling overwhelmed. Then, putting one foot in front of the other, we keep going.

Chapter 31

Yes, We Can

October 17

> *Things work out! Not all the time, but much of the time, and if we can keep that perspective, we are much less panicky and anxious. Why worry in anticipation of what might never be? Whatever will happen, will happen. The rest is attitude, and we can choose to be optimistic and have a happier life experience.*

Sometimes the problems of the world seem so big, and we seem so small, that it feels like there is nothing we can do that will make a difference. Whatever we believe and would like to see happen, there are powerful players pushing the other way, blocking any movement in our direction. Our hopes and wishes are thwarted by forces so massive that our actions barely slow them down if they are noticed at all. It's easy to despair and to feel like nothing we do matters. It's easy to give up and to believe that since we can't make a difference, we shouldn't bother trying.

The problems we face are daunting. A virus is confining us to our homes, limiting our interactions, damaging our livelihoods, threatening our health, and making us fearful for our lives. Our lives have been altered by the pandemic, and we can't seem to make it go away. Similarly, many people are facing a frightening financial picture. Thousands have lost their jobs, first temporarily, but now permanently, profits are down, real wages are down, government assistance is running out, debt is skyrocketing, and it's hard to see a happy ending before we encounter a whole lot of hardship. Once again, we feel helpless.

The very fabric of society seems to be stretching and fraying, and it feels like there is nothing we can do. Democracy is giving way to autocratic rulers who are answerable to no one. Economic inequality is getting more extreme, and social unrest is following closely in its footsteps. Societies are becoming increasingly polarized, with people viewing their neighbors as enemies and breaking ties with those who hold opposing viewpoints. We listen only to people who tell us what we already believe, tune into news sources that show us what we want to see, and stop looking critically at what is going on around us. We tolerate unacceptable behavior from people we support and wall ourselves in, viewing outsiders with hostility.

And on a planetary scale, fires, hurricanes, floods, and other disasters are everyday news. The Earth is warming, species are going extinct, and our very existence feels uncertain.

To overcome our despair, it's helpful to remember that we are a resourceful species, and that this is not the first time we've been in trouble. We can expand our perspective to realize that change takes time, and just like it took years for us to get in this mess, it will take time to get out of it. We can focus on the small and the local, asking ourselves what actions we can take personally to create positive impact for us and those around us. We should reach out and connect to others, especially those with opposing viewpoints, for in the end, if we sink, we all sink together. And we can never give up, despite the enormity of the task and all the setbacks. Can we fix it? Yes, we can.

Chapter 32

The "Uch" Factor

October 27

> *If we keep saying we've had a crazy day, are keeping insane hours, and are totally nuts with work, our adjectives might be telling us something! Let's heed their warning, slow down, and avoid losing our minds to unsustainable expectations.*

Sometimes we have to do something, and we just don't have the energy. We look at the task ahead and go, "Uch, not happening right now." And that's okay. Some tasks are unpleasant, annoying, or boring, and we don't feel like doing them. But lately, it seems like more things are falling into this category. Simple things seem complicated, tasks that used to be a breeze now require energy, and routine problems seem insurmountable. We grind slowly from one draining task to the next, with fewer rays of sunshine and joy peeking through the clouds than we remember from before.

When the "Uch" factor becomes pervasive in our lives, we need to start looking at our surroundings, our choices, and our internal narratives. It's not normal to feel like we're wading through quicksand all the time, and we might not be able to simply power our way to the other side.

The current environment is challenging. A worldwide pandemic has put us all on edge, making us worry for our health, our livelihood, and the very fabric of our society. Political and social strife accentuate a sense of greater divisions between people. Democracy is struggling all over the world, autocrats consolidate control, and income disparities widen. Companies are going out of business left and right, and food insecurity is growing for many people. And as the weather cools, the virus is multiplying and infecting more people, with hospitalizations and deaths to follow. How can we not be overwhelmed?

Work and home feel more stressful now. We are scrambling to meet our obligations on too many fronts at once, and everywhere there is worry. Are our loved ones going to be okay? Is our boss or customer happy? What did I forget to do today? Whom did I disappoint? We write to-do lists and add items faster than we can cross them off, trying to juggle our many obligations. Sometimes we just want to crawl back under the covers and yell "Stop the ride! I want to get off!" No wonder simple things seem darn near impossible to do.

But we do have choices. We can learn to turn down additional work when we've gotten overloaded. We can select which opportunities to pursue and which ones to let go. Sometimes more isn't better – it's just more. Sometimes the combination of too many good things in our lives is no longer good. We need to ask for help and give to others.

We can also manage the stories we tell ourselves. We should do our best but then refrain from judging ourselves harshly when we fall short of our expectations. We are not failures when we falter. We should be kind to ourselves and keep looking forward. Feeling overwhelmed all the time is a sign that we've taken a wrong turn. To improve the quality of our lives, we need to heed the warnings, take actions to slow down and regroup, and let go of what we don't control.

Chapter 33

Do Something Crazy

November 2

> *Sometimes you try every key, but the gate still won't open. Before you give up and walk away, consider climbing over it, or squeezing under, or knocking and seeing if someone might open it for you from the inside. The first gate to overcome is the one in your mind.*

My friend and I went kayaking today just outside Boston, in November, under cloudy skies. We unloaded the kayaks, trudged down to the river over a light covering of snow, and slid them into the water. It felt crazy given the snowfall this weekend, the sub-freezing overnight temperatures, and the likelihood of hypothermia if we fell in, but it was also a lot of fun. Alone on the river, save for the geese, ducks, and occasional swan, we floated past brown, snow-dusted woods and fields. We rode the currents under bridges, floated serenely through broad, shallow ponds, ducked under low-hanging branches, and encountered a beaver and a few grey herons. Three hours later, our journey ended just as the skies opened up and started pelting river and road alike with a cold November rain, right under the wire, more lucky than smart. Going kayaking today was not an obvious choice, but it was also medicine for the soul during troubled times, carving out an oasis of calm away from the cacophony and stress of our lives.

We need to step outside our normal routines and do something crazy once in a while. While taking precautions to ensure that we don't harm ourselves or others, we should invite our imaginations to come up with creative ways of combatting cabin fever and build our resilience for the days to come. We can do that thing we've wanted to do but never thought we would. We can challenge ourselves to learn new things and grow our skills, to explore areas of interest that we never had time for before.

This is a time of unprecedented challenges. The pandemic has impacted us all, regardless of the infection rate in our neighborhood. People are getting sick and dying at rates unheard of in a century, travel and commerce have virtually shut down, and the seams that hold our society together are straining under the pressure. Instead of banding together and regarding the virus as a common threat, we treat each other as the enemy and argue over whether the virus is really a problem. We hunker down in our echo chambers and are slowly losing our collective minds.

We can help ourselves by going outside our normal bounds, drawing outside the lines and taking some chances that we've been reluctant to take before. If we've always wanted to get a dog, but something has held us back, now might be the time to take the plunge and get one. If we've been unhappy in our jobs and now find ourselves at home, this might be the time to explore a new career. If we've always dreamed of running a marathon, we could start to train today. While we need to be responsible, stay healthy, and keep food on the table, we can also benefit by following our imaginations, even as they lead us into a small boat on an ice-cold river through the snowy woods.

Chapter 34

Everything is Conversation

November 7

> *The common denominator of leadership, negotiation, influence, and conflict resolution is communication, and in particular, our ability to listen to others with curiosity and empathy.*

Many things in life are scary. Whether we are facing a tough negotiation with an adversary, a public speaking engagement in front of an audience, a new leadership position at work, or any other difficult interaction, the very thought of it can be daunting. As a result, we often avoid these situations as long as we can, rush our way through them when we can no longer avoid, tense up, and underperform. One problem is that we think of these things as "things" - special types of activities that require extraordinary skills and talents. We imagine ourselves in the hot seat, the spotlight, with all eyes upon us, scoring our performance and criticizing our abilities. No wonder we panic!

But we can rewrite this script if we learn to regard these and all other interactions as conversations in which we both give and take with others. Conversations aren't as scary as these other interactions. After all, we've been engaged in conversations with those around us since the day we learned how to talk, and in some ways, even before that. Conversations aren't about us and our performance but instead about our connection with the other person or people, and therefore don't evoke the same performance anxiety in us.

For example, we can view negotiations as a contest of wills or battle of wits between opponents bent on overwhelming and undermining each other, but we can also choose to see negotiations as conversations where people with different needs and viewpoints resolve their differences and find solutions that meet their objectives. By reframing negotiations as conversations, we reduce the pressure on ourselves and focus instead on learning the needs of the other party. We slow down, become more relaxed and creative, and get out of our own way as we work things out with the other person.

Similarly, public speaking terrifies us because we think of it as a performance. All eyes are on us as we try to inspire, persuade, teach, or entertain our audience. But if we consider that like us, the people in audience are more concerned about themselves than they are about us, and that our goal is to connect with them rather than to impress them, we once again turn down the heat on ourselves. We look out at the audience and catch someone's eye, see them nod or smile in affirmation, and continue the conversation.

Even leadership can be thought of as a conversation. To inspire, we look for ways of connecting with our followers, and we do so more by listening than talking. We coach people through a combination of inquiry and advocacy, and we gain buy-in to our ideas by engaging with people's values and motivations. By reframing the challenging interactions in our life as conversations, we can reduce our stress, increase our effectiveness, and even have some fun.

Chapter 35

No Easy Answers

November 18

> *Life feels like a video game sometimes. Every time we master a level and feel good, a new level opens up and we're scrambling again, trying to figure things out as we go along.*

When times are tough, we look for easy answers and simple solutions. Why are we in the middle of a pandemic? "Simple – the Chinese did this to us," or "Simple – it's what we get for destroying the environment and encroaching on habitats," or "Simple – we were bad and God is punishing us." Similarly, when we look for solutions, we do the same thing. What's the answer to the pandemic? "Easy – we should all wear masks," or "Easy – we should develop a vaccine," or "Easy – we should pray for the pestilence to end." The complex realities of the situation and the incredible difficulty in finding a way out of it are just too much for us to handle, so we reach for explanations and remedies that are within our grasp.

But the fact that we can't deal with a complex reality doesn't change the nature of that reality. The pandemic began, spread, and developed into a devastating world-wide phenomenon through a series of complex and overlapping circumstances, some of which we might never understand with certainty. If the virus first occurred in bats, what exact path did it take before infecting the first human? What other species were involved? Why were some areas hit harder than others? Why do some people get sicker than others, at times seemingly randomly, and why do some people heal quickly and completely while others develop bizarre and unpredictable long-term effects? We're uncomfortable not knowing, and we want clear, straightforward explanations.

With no end in sight, we are equally flummoxed in charting our course of action. In the short-term, we can try to minimize infection by staying away from each other, wearing masks, and washing hands. But these actions can cause devastating economic, social, and psychological consequences. Meanwhile, we develop better therapeutics and medical processes to minimize deaths and serious complications, even as our hospitals overflow and our medical personnel are overstretched beyond their capacity to function. While we are hearing positive news regarding vaccines, we don't know their effectiveness over time, longer-term side effects, to whom and how they will be distributed and in what order, who will pay for them, and whether enough people will get them to bring about sufficient immunity in the community. There are so many parameters and so many open questions, while we want someone to tell us the simple answer.

If we want to defeat this virus, we must accept the complexity of the situation and embrace a comprehensive approach to designing the way forward. We must acknowledge that some of the history might never become clear to us and accept that the future is uncertain, likely riddled with both successes and setbacks. We must let our scientists and doctors lead the way both in explaining what has happened and in designing therapeutic treatments and vaccines. And we must resist the temptation of easy answers or blind belief in simple explanations. They got us to where we are, and we need a new way out.

Chapter 36

Life Changing Moments

November 22

> *Sometimes we look at something we've seen many times before and discover something about it we never knew existed, and it's like someone gave us a new toy. Never lose the wonder!*

Much of the time, life moves in a tranquil manner, one day flowing into the next. Every day provides new challenges and opportunities, which together, over time, shape our experience, but most days don't feel remarkable in their own right. Especially now, in the midst of a pandemic, the days have started to blend into one another, as we hunker down at home, walk around our familiar neighborhoods, and interact with a limited group of people. We've started forgetting which day is which as our work and home lives merge into a stream of virtual meetings.

But despite the monotony, there are notable days and life changing moments, and we ought to pay attention to them. Some of these moments are global in their nature – a natural disaster, an election result, a scientific discovery or technological invention, the outbreak of war or declaration of peace. We might remember where we were and what we were doing during one of these moments – glued to our screens or listening to repeated broadcasts of the event: horrified, excited, curious, riveted in some way.

Some moments are more localized, impacting our immediate environment rather than the whole world – our company reorganizes and lays off a friends or colleagues, our school transitions to remote teaching, a water main breaks, causing minor flooding and disrupting our lives for a week. While these events may not affect a large number of people, their impact on us can be significant. We spend most of our time within a small sphere, and anything that happens within that sphere casts a longer shadow on our lives.

Some of the most life changing moments are the ones that happen to us directly rather than to our environment. These might include the birth of a child, the death of a loved one, completion of a degree, the first day on a new job, a fire or accident, a chance meeting with a celebrity, or a date that marks the beginning of a new relationship. Since these events happen to us personally, they can change the quality of our experiences and impact our outlook on life.

There are life-changing moments when nothing happens at all, save for what goes on inside our minds. We have a new idea or solve a problem that we've been stuck on for a while. We discover something new or gain a new perspective we were lacking earlier. As John Steinbeck said, "I wonder how many people I have looked at all my life and never seen." We might even need to be the agents that bring these moments about, focusing our attention and opening our minds to new ideas. Routines are comfortable, but if we pay attention, we can gain a richer and more meaningful experience by noticing and appreciating our life-changing moments.

Chapter 37

The Marshmallow Test

November 29

> *Reading the instructions before opening the box and engaging with the product is a really smart thing to do. I wish I did it more often, but alas, it's so much fun to just open the box and start playing with things.*

In the 1960s, Stanford professor Walter Mischel conducted experiments on delayed gratification, observing children's ability to forego an immediate treat for a later benefit. Children were brought into a room and presented with a marshmallow. They were then told that the researcher would be back in a few minutes, and if they had not eaten the marshmallow, they would then get two. In the 1980s and 1990s, additional papers were published looking at a correlation between the children's ability to hold off eating the marshmallow and later success on the SATs and in their careers. While much of that correlation has since come into question, there is still merit to the idea that the ability to delay immediate gratification can have long term benefits.

If we put some of our money into a retirement account when we are young rather than spend it all on fun and fancy, then we will be able to retire in comfort later on in life. If we delay our fun and do our homework on Friday after school, we will have the whole weekend to enjoy ourselves without stress. Over and over again, we can find examples where we can benefit by delaying gratification, but it is so difficult to do in practice. Why? The temptation of immediate satisfaction is often overwhelming.

Now, we find ourselves in a global pandemic that has sickened millions and killed hundreds of thousands. In principal, fighting the virus shouldn't be that difficult. We need to stay away from each other, wear masks in public, avoid touching our faces, and wash our hands frequently and thoroughly. In reality, fighting the virus has been very difficult because it involves a whole lot of don'ts. Don't gather with your friends and family. Don't go out to restaurants and bars. Don't celebrate your holidays as you normally would. Like Mischel's researchers in the 1960s, the authorities are asking us to delay the immediate gratification of having life feel more normal in order to gain the benefit of having life actually go back to normal after we eradicate the virus.

Over and over again, with a few notable exceptions, as a species, we are failing this marshmallow test. We hate the feel of masks, so we choose not to wear them. We miss seeing our friends, so we go out to parties. We are a social species, and we try to get together with other people, believing that the consequences can't be too bad. But the end result is that the pandemic has dragged on, with each wave killing and sickening more of us. In our desire to put the pandemic behind us, we act in ways that make it longer and more severe. The situation is clearly more complex and involved than this, and there are many people who have no choice but to put themselves in harm's way, but the rest of us have choices and should heed the lessons of the marshmallow test.

Chapter 38

Beyond Marshmallows

December 6

> *I tried the marshmallow test on my cat this morning. I gave him half a cup of food and explained that if he ate it slowly, he would get another one in the evening. He promptly gobbled down the whole thing and threw up on the carpet. First, I thought, "silly cat," but then I had to confess that I had set him up to fail.*

The 1960s marshmallow test experiment correlated children's ability to delay gratification their future success. While delaying gratification can have long term benefits, it is dangerous to draw conclusions based on this test. Many factors impact behavior, and we should not judge people based on whether, as children, they ate the marshmallow or waited for the researcher to return. More generally, we should be careful before we draw conclusions about people based on any observed behavior.

For example, children might have come in more or less hungry, depending on when they had last eaten. If our belly is full, it is easier to delay dessert, while if we are famished, the marshmallow in front of us meets an immediate need. Similarly, looking at the pandemic, it's easy to condemn people who attend social gatherings, but not all of us are in the same circumstances. Some of us have family members nearby or can connect with others electronically, while others live in isolation and suffer crushing loneliness. Instead of judging these people, we should try to understand their needs and provide safer venues for them to interact.

Another factor in the marshmallow experiment involved the home environment. Children from single-child homes might expect to find a dessert still available if they waited, while those who grew up with siblings might expect it to be gone if they waited. If we are accustomed to scarcity and vanishing opportunities, the marshmallow test is no longer valid for us. During the early part of the pandemic, hoarding of some products led to shortages that didn't really make sense, but rather than condemn the behavior, we could instead have tried to reassure the public and provide additional supplies.

Finally, children from stable, nurturing homes and safe communities might trust that the researcher would come back with another marshmallow while children surrounded by an environment of distrust wouldn't. Similarly, societies exhibit different levels of trust in their governments, and even within a society, different people have more or less reason to believe in the authorities. The politicization of the pandemic and conflicting messages from leaders have further undermined this trust. It is therefore up to leaders at all levels to act with integrity, to be careful and consistent in their communication, and to respond with empathy and understanding to people who distrust government proclamations and actions.

Judging others based on perceived behavior is easy but unfair, while an effective response is much more nuanced. We must go beyond a simplistic interpretation of the marshmallow test.

Chapter 39

Every Day

December 14

> *You have no flaws, only features. If you are impatient, channel your energy into intensity. If you are unable to focus on one thing, work on several things at once. If you feel anxious, write down your thoughts. However you operate, work with yourself and don't think of yourself as lacking.*

Every day presents us with decisions, and the way we respond impacts our accomplishments, interactions with others, and the quality of our lives. We must decide between our long-term happiness and our short-term satisfaction, between doing for others or only for ourselves, between things that build up our capacities and things that erode us over time. We struggle with these choices, and many times end up going the wrong way, in directions that we later regret. And even if we prevail and can look back with satisfaction at the choices we made yesterday, today is a new day, filled with similarly agonizing contradictions like a never-ending treadmill.

The cycle of making decisions, living through the consequences, and facing an equally daunting set of decisions the next day erodes our will and saps our strength. Whether we are trying to focus on our work, exercise and eat right, or be mindful in our interactions with others, we get ground down and exhausted by unrelenting forces pushing us in the other direction. We procrastinate and avoid meaningful tasks because they are more difficult than fun activities that provide us with immediate satisfaction.

We try to overcome our need for instant gratification with willpower, forcing ourselves to exercise, sitting down to do our work, closing the fridge after opening it for the seventh time for no good reason, but in the end, we lose the battle. We eat that brownie, play that video game, take that nap, and do what makes us feel good in the moment, knowing that not so far down the road we will feel bad about it. It turns out that willpower is simply ineffective as a method of counteracting our short-term impulses. Our short-term needs are powerful and relentless, and even if we can hold them off with willpower for a short while, our resolve gets eroded over time, and all they need is a moment of weakness to push us into a decision we regret.

A more effective way to manage our decisions is to change our setting and develop different habits – as Thaler and Sunstein suggested in their book, to Nudge ourselves into better choices. If working in the dining room makes it too difficult to avoid the fridge every time our work gets frustrating, maybe we should try to work upstairs in a different room or go to the office. If we play on our phone in bed for an hour every morning, maybe we can put the phone out of reach when going to sleep. Journaling our decisions and getting support from others can also help us stay on track. Finally, we need to forgive ourselves our past transgressions and move on. No matter what we did yesterday, today is a new day full of new choices.

Chapter 40

Time

December 19

> *Another Friday night has almost run its course. Another week has ended. The days are long, but the weeks go by quickly, and like them go the months and years. Life is short! Make the moments count.*

Time is our most precious commodity. Since we are all doomed to die sometime, our days are numbered, and there are only so many hours in each one. It therefore makes sense that we try to make our days count and make best use of the time we have. In an effort to do this, we might set grand goals for ourselves, overload ourselves with tasks and obligations, structure our hours with checklists and apps, and try to multitask and do the impossible. We might treat our lives as a race to the finish, knowing that ultimately, it will be a race we lose, and judge ourselves harshly in light of all the things we failed to accomplish.

Alternatively, we could ignore time, letting our days flow one into the next without achieving much of anything, following the path of least effort. We might work when we need to, sleep when we can, eat when we are able, and look for ways to kill time from the moment we open our eyes each day to the moment we shut them at night. More likely, we might simply focus on getting through our day, putting food on the table, taking care of others, doing our jobs, maintaining our homes, suffering through the grind as we struggle to meet our obligations, and go to bed exhausted in anticipation of repeating the cycle. Many of us simply don't have the luxury of controlling our time but are at the mercy of circumstance in how we structure our days.

How then do we make sense of time, neither racing nor lazing, or simply being swept along with the flow? How do we make our very limited time on this Earth meaningful, no matter our circumstances, and what does that even mean? How can we measure our success? To find meaning, we should first consider what we care about. We might be motivated by helping others, being creative, gaining wealth, learning something new, connecting with people, taking care of our families, or improving the world. If we gain clarity regarding our values, we can then try to live our lives as consistently as possible with those values.

Time is finite, so everything we choose to do implies selecting something else not to do. Where we can, we should question the obligations on our lists, since some are placed upon us by circumstance and others are self-imposed. Is everything we are doing really that important? Does it optimize the quality of our days based on what matters most to us? If we tend to overload ourselves and treat life as a race, perhaps we can do less rather than more, and focus on the most important things. Some time we might choose to do nothing at all, giving ourselves time to rest and reflect. Someday we will approach the end of the journey and want to look back, without regrets, at how we spent our time.

Chapter 41

Resistance to Change

December 26

> *When your world gets turned upside down, don't lament the good old days when it was right side up. Instead, think how cool it is that you can stand on the ceiling, see things from a new perspective, and discover opportunities you couldn't even imagine before.*

We are an adaptable species, and that adaptability has allowed us to expand from the savannas of Africa to the frozen tundra of the Arctic and from the arid cliffs near the Dead Sea to the towering peaks of the Himalayas. And yet, when confronted with change, many of us respond with fear, avoid and delay it as long as we can, resist and grumble when there's no longer a choice, and grieve for happier days when things seemed more familiar.

For many years, we have tolerated numerous flaws in our work environment. We suffered long commutes to work, accepting the concept of rush hour, sitting for hours on congested highways or packed into trains and busses. We suffered first in cubicles and then in open offices under harsh florescent lights, trying to manage the distractions around us and appear productive to our peers and managers. Concerned about face-time and office politics, it was difficult for us to be at our best or to make a meaningful impact on our clients and coworkers.

Our home lives and our work lives disconnected, and our cities became hollow spaces full of glass buildings that emptied in the early evening while we battled traffic on our way to quieter and more affordable spaces. The bulk of our days were spent commuting and working, leaving less and less time for our families or for healthy downtime. All that traffic contributed to smog, and those office towers raised the price of real estate, making life in the city unaffordable for most and less pleasant for many.

Some of us noticed these things and called for change, advocating for work-at-home policies or flexible hours, more bike lanes and better, faster trains. Over and over again, we were rebuffed. We were told that remote work would kill company culture and productivity. It was commonly understood that there was no substitute for face-to-face meetings, and that it made sense for us to fly across the country for a two-hour project meeting with a client. Yes, commuting was a pain, but we really needed everyone in at nine and out at five or there would be chaos.

Then change was thrust upon us. A virus caused us to abandon our offices, limit our contact with others, and minimize our travel. The most conservative, stodgiest companies, that had previously refused to contemplate remote work, suddenly found themselves running entirely from homes, with workers communicating via phone or video. Not only did the sky not fall, but productivity was often enhanced. We translated commuting into greater output while also gaining family and recreation time. We learned to cook and garden and ride bikes, while still closing deals and getting our work done.

Someday, hopefully soon, the pandemic will pass, and personal contact will resume. While many of us will go back to the office, some of the changes will stick and help us live more productive, happier, and sustainable lives.

Chapter 42

Gratitude

January 1

> *If we can find something to be thankful for every day, even in our least cheery moments; if we can hold onto gratitude for the little things, we become masters of our life experience rather than victims of our misfortunes.*

Life can be very challenging sometimes. When we encounter difficulties, it's natural for us to feel exhausted, become embittered, and adopt a negative perspective on the world. If, at those times, someone were to suggest to us to adopt a practice of gratitude, we might look at them strangely and wonder what they're talking about. Forcing ourselves to feel thankful at times when we are feeling put upon can feel artificial and useless. Even trying to list items for which we are grateful can seem strange. Do we go with mundane activities such as being alive or breathing? Do we focus on more specific little moments where something good happened within the overall picture of a dark and dreary time? Having tried such practices in the past, my experience was that they never really clicked with me, and I felt like I was merely going through the motions.

Then, out of the blue, my mother got sick and eventually passed away. I remember those last few days, walking across the parking lot into the hospital, breathing in the cool spring air while my mother lay connected to machines in her ICU bed. I started noticing the quality of light in the morning sun, the sound of the wind through the leaves, the sensation of the sun's warmth on my skin. Suddenly, every tree seemed remarkable and every bird beautiful, as I became hyper-aware of the contrast between what I was experiencing outside and what my mother was missing in her final few days. It's been nearly 15 years since that time, but the feeling has never left me and has only grown over the years. A close encounter with deprivation and death made me grateful for the little things that I take for granted every day.

I realized that like many things, gratitude begins with awareness. We grow up in our bodies and surroundings, and naturally assume that things have always been the way they are and will continue into the future. But this is an illusion. We are all one step away from calamity and one stroke of bad luck from oblivion. Like the antelope grazing calmly on the plain one moment only to be some carnivore's dinner minutes later, we are often unaware at how precarious everything is. Life is full of risks, and whether it be an accident, our health, a global pandemic, or a financial crisis, much of our fate lies outside our control. Sure, we should eat right and exercise and look both ways before we cross the street, but at the end of the day, we are simply lucky to be alive and have the things we have. With this awareness, gratitude comes easily. Thus fortified, we can strive to be our best and hope for even better things ahead.

Chapter 43

Happy New Year

January 10

> *The cold of winter can help us appreciate the coming spring. Otherwise, we might take the nice weather for granted. The pandemic can likewise help us appreciate all the wonderful things we have in and around our lives during normal times. We probably take too many of them for granted as well.*

This is a time of year when we wish each other a Happy New Year. While the first of January is an artificial marker of time, similar to holidays and birthdays, it is never-the-less an opportunity for us to take stock of the year that just passed and to articulate our hopes for the year to come. In light of this reckoning, we often set goals for ourselves and resolve to change our lives in some way, sometimes successfully but often less so, as the challenge of sustained effort wears down our will.

Ten days into 2021, the new year is looking more like a continuation of 2020 than like a fresh start. The pandemic, which defined most of the past year is raging across the planet more intensely than ever, shutting down entire countries, sickening millions, and killing thousands every day. The economy, having suffered a body blow last spring, was starting to recover over the summer and early fall, only to stagnate again in November, December, and now January.

Optimism Is A Choice

In the United States, the political stress accompanying the 2020 election was supposed to have ended in November, but then dragged on into December, culminating in destructive chaos during the first week in January. On the other side of the Atlantic, Brexit negotiations finally culminated in an agreement, only to usher in an indefinite period of uncertainty and additional negotiations. Across the world, democracy is in retreat, as nationalistic governments build walls, restrict the free press, limit individual freedoms, oppress minorities, and look to reclaim a mythical glorious past. The very fabric of society is strained, as we retreat into silos and echo chambers, seeing only what we want to believe and listening only to people who tell us what we want to hear.

And the big problems haven't gone away. Damage from natural disasters hit records as temperatures soared, devastating some areas with hurricanes and wildfires while baking others in droughts or drowning them in floods. Nuclear technology has proliferated, regional conflicts continue to simmer, and the world just feels like a more divided and dangerous place. Looking back at 2020 and now the start of 2021, it just seems like we're in for more of the same, and the transition from one year to the next doesn't seem that happy. At least so far.

And yet, it's essential that we greet each other with a Happy New Year, affirming that no matter what happened up until this moment, every day is a new day, and that the year ahead is one of possibilities. Vaccines might finally tame the pandemic, businesses and economies might revive, political instability might stabilize, and societal rifts might heal. We must choose to approach the new year with optimism and hope, endeavor to be our best selves, and reach out to each other.

Chapter 44

Curiosity

January 17

> *If we remain curious and open-minded, the universe will always invite us to ask more questions, and the journey will never be dull*

We are an inquisitive species. Set a small child free anywhere – a garden, a classroom, a beach, a museum, or a playground, and the child will start exploring. Teach the child to read, and that curiosity becomes boundless, investigating vast worlds through the printed word. And this curiosity doesn't need to end with childhood. As we grow and expand our horizons, we might extend our curiosity to new people and cultures, explore the mysteries of the world through science and mathematics, probe the workings of machinery by taking it apart and trying to put it back together. We experiment with new experiences.

But not all of us stay curious. Some of us develop fears of the unknown that limit our curiosity. We associate the familiar with comfort, the new with risk. We become creatures of habit, following the same routines day after day, walking only along well-trodden paths, eating only foods we've eaten before, and interacting only with people we already know. Over time, our world becomes smaller, and we build walls around ourselves to protect us from the scary unknown beyond.

For others of us, the limitations on curiosity originate not in fear but in attitude. We become judgmental, casting some things as good and others as bad, and shutting our eyes to anything beyond the artificial bounds we have created. Certain that our ideas are the only correct ones, we see no value in exploring the beliefs of others. Embracing our own culture, language, and nationality, we can't see the point in going elsewhere. Interacting only with people who look and sound like us, we immediately distrust and reject people who appear different and unfamiliar.

The internet was supposed to help remedy some of these behaviors by giving us instantaneous access to all of the information in the world, right at our fingertips. Social media was to be the great connector, allowing us to interact with, and therefore understand better, anyone and everyone everywhere. In theory, technology allows us to do these things by tearing down the barriers of time and space that isolated us from people far away across the planet. We no longer have an excuse for estrangement due to distance, language, time zones, or cultures. We are no longer limited to the information gathered in our homes or at our local library.

That was the theory, but in practice, we have used the internet to partition ourselves and restrict our curiosity to the familiar. We choose news sources that tell us what we already believe and interact only with friends and communities that already share our ideas. We spend hours on the internet, yet learn nothing new, and miss the opportunity to expand our horizons. Foregoing our natural curiosity is very sad, and also dangerous. To confront the challenges that threaten our wellbeing and survival, we need to regain our curiosity. We must overcome our fears, suspend our judgments, and explore the unknown.

Chapter 45

Words Without Consequences

January 23

> *Night falls whether or not we've gotten our work done, and morning comes regardless of whether we've slept. Accepting this reality may be annoying and difficult, but we must, because the Earth doesn't care, and will keep rotating no matter how we feel.*

We live in a world where words have no consequences, lies don't come home to roost, charlatans overrule the experts, and appearances matter more than facts. When someone first said that "a lie can travel halfway around the world while the truth is still putting on its shoes," the internet and social media didn't exist, and ideas traveled at the speed of a horse rather than the speed of light. Now, any belief, verifiable or fictional, can gain followers and widespread acceptance before we know if it's real. This has created a dangerous situation in which it becomes difficult for people to distinguish facts from hoaxes and reality from imagination.

Once a belief takes hold, we want to hold onto it, no matter how hard we have to work to reconcile it with conflicting information. In The Demon Haunted World, Carl Sagan imagines telling us that there's a fire breathing dragon in his garage. We come over to look at it, but see no dragon. He apologizes and remarks that he forgot to tell us that the dragon is invisible. When we offer to spread flour on the floor of the garage so we can see the dragon's footsteps, he then explains that the dragon floats in the air. No matter what method we devise to confirm the existence of the dragon, he comes up with an excuse as to why it wouldn't work. In the end, Sagan postulates that this whole conversation tells us more about his mental state than it does about the veracity of the dragon.

As ideas spread wildly without verification, we fall increasingly vulnerable to individuals and groups that seek to convince us of their theories and motivate us to actions that serve their ends. Any information we encounter that contradicts their theory is easily dismissed or explained away, just like the dragon, and the lies keep going. In addition, because we often confine ourselves to groups of like-minded people, we are not exposed to anyone whose beliefs differ from our own. That same internet, which was supposed to unite and connect us by giving us access to all of the information in the world is now dividing us more than ever, as we choose what information sources to watch and what people to connect to.

But in the end, truth does matter. The coronavirus doesn't care what we believe, and if we treat it like a hoax, it becomes our reality anyway, and people get hurt. To stop this cycle and expose the con-artists, we must connect to others, especially those who hold beliefs different from ours, and together demand rigorous proof of any theory or assertion. We must attach consequences to lies and hold people to account over their words, putting our faith neither in people or groups, but in facts that can be demonstrated and proven. Otherwise, reality will catch up to us and the price we end up paying may be high.

Chapter 46

Take the Day Off

January 30

> *It's amazing how much joy a small cup of ice cream can bring after a long, hard day of work. It's the little things that sometimes make all the difference to our quality of life.*

We have become a 24-7 society, tethered to our cell phones, working all hours of the day and night, saddled with worries and responsibilities on every front. We wake up already behind on our to-do lists for the day, rush from one activity to the next while constantly interrupted by external demands, and fall into bed exhausted but wired, tallying all the things we didn't get to and already constructing our lists for the next day. Our bodies shuffle along like zombies throughout the day while our minds are in overdrive, threatening to overheat in the scramble to stay on top of everything.

We need to learn how to stop and take a day off, to rest our minds and renew our bodies. It is an illusion, a fantasy, to think that if we just keep up the frenzy for a little longer, we will finally conquer our obligations and be able to rest. There are always new demands put upon us and new tasks to complete. Whether we work six, seven, or eight days a week, we will never finish the job and never find peace.

Every day, we grow older and more tired, and every mountain seems higher than the last. By never stopping to rest, we erode our capacity over time and actually become less effective, working harder but accomplishing less. We need to recognize this reality and look at the bigger picture of our lives. What are we neglecting by working so hard? How has our focus on the quantity of our accomplishments impacted the quality of our experience? When we have come to the end of the road, as invariably all of us will, what will we look back upon with regret?

The answer is not in becoming more efficient or doing more in less time, but instead in finding a balance between doing and not doing. On occasion, we need to sleep more and better, wake up to an empty list, allow ourselves the luxury of boredom, laugh with those around us, and be satisfied at having accomplished nothing. We need to slow down, connect with others, indulge in the unimportant, celebrate comfort, daydream, relax, and take a nap. We must carve out sacred times for rest or be overrun by our obligations. We must also find small moments, eddies in the stream, to recharge.

Letting go like this might be very difficult for some of us. We are fueled by anxiety, worried that if we don't keep running like mice in a wheel, something will go terribly wrong – things won't get done, and people might get hurt. But the world revolved before we were here and will continue to turn even if we take a moment for ourselves. So, let's take the day off, and then come back stronger, smarter, and ready to take on the world.

Chapter 47

Too Much Bad News

February 7

> *Be careful before mocking someone or something as a dinosaur. Dinosaurs dominated the planet for over 150 million years, which is way more than we've been around, and but for a rogue asteroid, might still be here today. Let's hope we do as well....*

The world is a fascinating place! Interesting things are happening all the time, and we can find out about them by tuning into the news. Now, more than ever, we can get news from anywhere any time we want, and we can even tailor our sources to ensure that the news we hear conforms to our beliefs. As the line blurs between news and commentary, news and entertainment, or news and advertising, we get drawn in deeper and can become immersed in a never-ending stream of information.

But no matter our views or politics, no matter our sources of information, some of the news we hear will make us happy, while other stories will be upsetting. As we scan through the headlines, we might feel our heartrate rise with indignation or anger as we come across events that contradict our moral convictions, upend our social norms, threaten our physical, emotional, or economic safety, or simply go against our wishes.

Over the past year, we have been battered by a global pandemic, economic uncertainty, political turmoil, and social unrest. It's no wonder that many of us are anxious, stressed and jumpy. Small things gain significance, as we peer at our devices with dread, waiting for the next upsetting bit of information. Not a week passes without news of a beloved celebrity or athlete passing, a coup or conflict erupting somewhere, a company closing its doors or laying off employees, or some other calamity that leaves us feeling vulnerable. Even the weather seems stressful.

Some of us have responded to this flood of scary news by becoming obsessive, scanning the news on our phones as we open our eyes in the morning, checking our favorite outlets many times a day, and signing off at night with one final glance to ensure that the sky hasn't fallen. No wonder we don't sleep well. Others of us have instead averted our eyes and shut our ears on the theory that if we don't know the news, we won't be as upset. We lock ourselves away and focus on our immediate surroundings, trying to insulate ourselves from the greater world while still secretly dreading what we don't know or understand.

Rather than obsess or hide, we might benefit from some perspective and healthy optimism. The news has always been mixed, and despite the good and bad, our planet, species, and society have persevered for a long time – clunked along, bruised and battered, but still here to talk about it. Not too far in the future, the news we fret about today will be history, fading quickly and barely remembered. Our triumphs and tragedies will be lost in the vastness of time, as were those that came before us and that bother us so little today. While accepting that some news can be upsetting, we can also choose to focus on the positives, noticing the everyday heroes that make the world a better place and appreciating our good fortune.

Chapter 48

A Light in the Distance

February 16

> *The toughest part of the race is when we start sprinting toward the finish line, only to realize we still have another lap to go....*

A year of pandemic feels like we've been driving through a long, dark tunnel, and while vaccines are giving us hope, we are a long way from done. When we first enter a tunnel and everything is dark, there's a moment of trepidation and excitement as our eyes adjust and we wonder what we are in for. How long will we be in there? Who else will be in there with us and what will they be doing? What exactly is above us, and how worried does that make us feel? While the tunnel makes us nervous, we might expect it to be short, and so to find ourselves on the other side in not too long a time, emerging into the bright sunshine to continue on our way.

If the tunnel turns out to be a long one, we become accustomed to the darkness, and plod on ahead. For the longest time it's hard to imagine that the tunnel will ever end. The initial fear subsides, only to be replaced by a mix of steady, low-level anxiety coupled with acceptance of the new normal. We know the tunnel will end sometime, and so we just keep going, some of us peering into the distance hoping for a glimmer, and others looking at our feet, unconcerned by the gloom. It feels like we've always been in the tunnel and always will be.

When we finally see a light in the distance, our heart jumps with hope that we are finally coming to the end of things. We get excited, and start moving faster, anticipating better times. But that little glimmer of light is elusive, as we realize how much tunnel is still left ahead of us. At such times, we must redouble our efforts and persevere, despite the disappointment. We are at the crossroads between excitement and despair, no longer numb, but not hopeful either. How then do we keep ourselves going? How do we sustain the effort when we are just so tired, and yet there is still so far to go? We need to simultaneously push forward toward our goal while also investing in self-care and shoring up our capacity to keep going at all. To help ourselves and others through this time, we need to maintain our stamina, nurture our souls, and take care of each other. We must connect with those around us, reflect and rest, exercise, focus on the positives, and look for ways to serve those who are struggling. When the pandemic first hit, we scrambled. Then as it dragged on, we plodded along. Now, with the end in sight but not yet here, we must persevere. We can't give up, can't get complacent, and need to keep focused on the goal. If we do these things, we can end this.

Chapter 49

Judgment Day

February 23

> *It is tempting to gloat when we have won the match, just as it is natural to resent the other team when we have lost, but in doing either, we taint ourselves and the game. We should celebrate our wins with empathy and mourn our loses with grace, treating our adversaries with respect and recognizing that tomorrow we might be in each other's shoes.*

Nowadays it seems like every day is judgment day. The rise of the internet and social media has made it very easy to criticize other people, and we are often invited to do so. Hardly a day passes when we are not asked to review a product, fill out an opinion survey, comment on someone else's ideas, or react to a post or picture. Watching Perseverance Mars rover descend down to the surface of Mars on NASA's website, it was hard not to be struck by the hundreds of comments pouring in by the second onto their feed, some congratulatory, others bizarre. Why do we feel compelled to judge or comment on everything? Is this good for us?

As every armchair quarterback demonstrates, it's much easier to judge than to do. From a safe vantage point away from the action, unaffected by the pressure of decision-making in real time, the perfect play seems obvious. "How could the quarterback miss the wide receiver, completely open down the field?" We yell at the screen, complain to our friends, and go on at length about how we could have done so much better. We apply the same formula to everything around us. We expect products that never fail, flawless customer service, and answers to every question. We demand from others a level of competence that we could never achieve ourselves.

And we go further. In our criticism of others, we go beyond judging their actions, and instead start commenting on their character, abilities, and overall worth. We call them names, criticize their appearance, make fun of their flaws, and invalidate them as humans. We have stopped cutting people any slack, and have tossed the golden rule to the side of the path. From the safe anonymity of our computers and phones, we have forgotten the pain that accompanies such judgment and are oblivious to the damage we cause.

But judging others harshly and relentlessly is not only harmful to them, but also damaging to us. In adopting a judgmental approach, we stop being curious and neglect to ask the questions that could inform our understanding. We become closed off to new approaches and different ideas, and reject things we don't understand. Our minds are built for bias, so we tend to see what we already believe. By judging everything, we predetermine our conclusions and close ourselves off to new information, often to our detriment.

Judgment has its place, and a society that can't critique itself is just as likely to be doomed as one that judges relentlessly. But judgement should be a destination rather than a starting point. By adopting a curious stance, we first endeavor to observe what's in front of us, with as little bias as we can muster. We ask questions and try to understand with an open mind. By perceiving first, the judgements we come to are better informed, kinder, more constructive, and healthier for everyone. Not every day needs to be judgment day.

Chapter 50

Lessons from the Weather

March 3

> *No matter what has come before, the mistakes we made and the places where we stumbled and fell, the road ahead is unknown, so we might as well expect good things. No matter how rough the path, how thick the brambles, how steep the mountain, or how deep the quicksand, we can only get through them if we believe that we can. And throughout it all, we might try to enjoy the journey, make memories, and have a great story to tell when we are through.*

Last weekend I went kayaking in the Charles River. This in itself would not have been significant had it not been February, when kayaking should have been impossible in Boston. Indeed, one week earlier, the river was frozen over, and people were out skating. Now, after a week of warm rain, it was 50 degrees and nothing but open water.

Excited, I took my outdoor plants, which have been hibernating in the house over the last few months, out to my front stairs for some much-appreciated fresh air and sunshine. "March begins tomorrow," I thought, "and spring is around the corner." By Monday night, I brought them back inside, as the temperature plummeted to ten degrees. Looking ahead, temperatures will vacillate between the 50s and the teens over the next ten days, with swings of thirty degrees within 24 hours. Spring is coming, but winter is not letting go either.

One year into the pandemic, I can't help but notice parallels. With the vaccines, spring is coming, but the pandemic winter is not done with us yet. Infection rates are stubbornly high, new variants are developing, and people are getting sick and dying. Like my plants, we have been hibernating indoors, isolated from each other, and are eager for the fresh air of companionship and the sunshine of fun. But like my plants, we are also vulnerable, and if we fail to manage conditions carefully, we could get hurt.

So, how do we respond to this confusing time, whipsawing between spring and winter, hope and vulnerability? First, we need to gather information and make data-based decisions. It was no secret to me that the temperature was dropping on Monday night. I had looked at the forecast and could choose an appropriate course of action. There is a lot of data out there about infection rates, safety precautions, and the relative risk of various activities. We just need to look at the data and make informed decisions. Pretending and hoping don't change reality.

Second, we need to gain perspective by looking into the past and toward the future. I can look back at weather patterns over the past few years in Boston as well as the volatility of the past few months, and also have the benefit of a ten-day forecast looking ahead. Looking at the data from the last year, other pandemics, and scientific predictions for the next few weeks, we can also make strategic decisions to guide our behavior.

Finally, we should take care of our bodies, minds, and souls by engaging in rewarding activities, but we should take precautions as we do so. Kayaking was like medicine for me, but I also wore a life jacket, carried a sealed bag with dry clothes, and avoided dangerous areas. We can see each other safely, do things we enjoy, but must continue to adhere to safe practices. Spring is coming, but only by recognizing that winter is still here, will we herald the arrival of summer.

Chapter 51

Jethro the Consultant

March 10

> *Don't put off till tomorrow what you can put off forever! Life is a lot nicer if we simplify, delegate, and eliminate unnecessary items entirely.*

Management consultants have been dispensing advice for thousands of years. In Exodus, it is said that in the desert, Moses sat in judgment before the people from morning until evening, because the entire nation wanted his advice. His father in law, Jethro, observed what was going on and advised Moses that what he's doing isn't sustainable; that he will wilt and the nation with him if he keeps trying to do all of the work on his own. Jethro advises Moses to appoint subordinates, who can take care of the routine matters, while Moses attends to the big, important matters. Thus, began the field of management consulting, and the first words of wisdom from Jethro the consultant involved delegation.

Since that time, consultants have continued advising managers to delegate, but unlike Moses, many of us have resisted this advice. We know better than to try to do everything ourselves, and yet many of us can't resist the temptation. Intellectually, we understand the benefits of delegation so why is it so difficult for us to let go, to select and train our team members and then to devolve some of the work to these qualified people?

Some of us struggle due to a need for control. Deep down, we believe that if we don't do everything ourselves, it won't be done to our standard, and then something bad will happen. Our need for control belies arrogance, fear, and needless perfectionism – arrogance, in thinking that only we can do the work, fear that something will go wrong, and needless perfectionism in wanting everything to be done precisely as we imagine. For the most part, we could let go of all three. There is ample evidence that much of the work could be accomplished by others, that most errors aren't disastrous, and that our way isn't the only good way.

Others of us refrain from delegating because training others is time-consuming and error-prone. Even though delegation pays off over time, getting other people up to speed slows us down. We know we should train someone to do a task, but it's much easier just to do it ourselves. When we train someone new, the task takes longer to accomplish, while we can't get our own work done. In addition, the new person is likely to make mistakes, which we will have to spend time correcting.

To delegate, we must first manage our fears and then shift our perspective. Then, by letting go and bringing others along, we expand our capacity, free ourselves to tackle meaningful challenges, and create more sustainable and resilient processes. Thank you, Jethro, for your advice. Now we need to start listening to it.

Chapter 52

Milestones

March 14

Make your days count, because they are countable.

For good or bad, we humans like to mark time in milestones. A year and one week ago, we went into lockdown and the world turned inside out. One year ago, today, I wrote my first weekly article, and this is my fifty second. I haven't seen one of my children in over fourteen months and another in eleven months. It's been thirteen months since I've taken a flight, and over a year since I've sat inside a restaurant, seen a play, or entered a friend's house. It's been an interesting year, replete with challenges and discoveries, in which the normal has become a distant memory and the unimaginable has become normal.

Even time has gone sideways this year, simultaneously slowing down, speeding up, and becoming blurry. On one hand, the pandemic feels stretched out and seems to extend endlessly both into the past and the future. Days and months go by, and despite the hope of vaccination, the dread of infection hovers over us like smog on a sunny day. On the other hand, our worlds have shrunk around us, isolated in our homes, with routines and obligations making the hours run into each other. Every week seems to end minutes after it starts. As my personal and professional life have intertwined, my daily schedule has become a salad of activities. I've met clients remotely at 5 AM this year as well as at midnight, stopped midday to help a kid with school, and gave up on having uninterrupted time to think. On the other hand, napping has become a possibility.

Time is an abstract concept. Despite that, I am keenly aware of its passage, marking the days by observing the sun as it rises and sets on the horizon, the weeks as they cycle between workdays and weekends, the months in the phases of the moon, and the years by the ages of my kids. Milestones also enhance this awareness, as I note births, deaths, anniversaries, birthdays, holidays, national and international events, and personal moments. While all such numbers are arbitrary, somehow, they feel significant.

Why do we notice time so much, and why this obsession with milestones? Perhaps one reason is because in the end, we know that the number of days between the moment we are born and the moment we die are finite and countable. Assigning significance to milestones helps us attach meaning to our activities and accomplishments. Conversely, perhaps the reason is that we can't fully grasp the concept of time and our place in the universe, and marking down milestones helps us translate the abstract into concrete terms we can manage. Regardless of the reasons, we like milestones, and one year into the pandemic, this one seems worth noting.

Chapter 53

Both And

March 26

> *Snow is on the ground, but spring is in the air. If we learn to live with and celebrate the contradictions in ourselves and all around us, we might forego the need to be judgmental and can become more curious and excited instead.*

Confronted by tough issues, we often divide ourselves into opposing camps, taking positions that seem contradictory and incompatible. Over the past year, as humanity has grappled with a worldwide pandemic, we have seen some people declare that we must focus on defeating the virus at all costs, even if it means locking down our cities and shutting down our economies, while others have insisted that we must preserve our economies, even at the cost of a less effective response to the pandemic. It's either or, saving lives or saving the economy, death by disease or death by starvation and despair.

Only it's not! Some nations have succeeded in managing both the virus and the economy and have done so by first questioning the false dichotomy that says it can't be done. By aiming for eradication of the virus rather than just suppressing its rate of infection down to a lower level, these countries have managed to return their lives to nearly normal and their economies back to growth. Their response was severe and locally painful, but also effective in preventing the virus from spreading through their communities, and after the localized outbreaks were isolated and extinguished, it was back to business as usual. By contrast, countries that persisted in perpetuating the narrative of dichotomies have continued to limp along with high rates of infection and death, and faltering economies.

The pandemic is hardly the only facet of our lives where we portray things as contradictory to each other when they may actually coexist. Must we really choose between supporting business development and preserving the environment? Is there really a contradiction between loving our country and disagreeing with the policies of our government? Can the prosperity of a company really come only at the expense of its labor force? Shouldn't it be possible for us to love our families but also to love our time alone without them? If we can catch ourselves before we get drawn into false dichotomies or manage to catch a lifeline out of them after the fact, then we can make better decisions and, perhaps, be happier in the process.

To succeed, we can start with the premise that the dichotomies we perceive are simply narratives in our own minds, and like any narratives, are ours to rewrite. All of these ideas, and the relation between them, are merely constructs that we create using our imaginations as a way of making sense of the world. All of them can and should be questioned. While invoking simplified models can help us to understand issues and make decisions, approaching the world with a black and white, us and them, right and wrong mentality can also polarize us and lead us to very damaging conclusions. Sometimes, it's both and, not either or.

Chapter 54

The Optimistic Lifestyle

April 4

> *We should try to find the humor in every situation. It may not change things, but it will change how we experience them for the better.*

My father has always referred to me as an optimist, and always sarcastically. What he really meant is that I always imagine I can fit more things into the time allotted than are realistically possible, and that therefore I'm always running late. It's true, of course. I am always running late, and I often try to do too much, but I'll take his designation as an optimist and own it happily. A year ago, I wrote that optimism is a choice. Now, I'll go further and suggest that optimism is a lifestyle. The choices we make over time accumulate, and if we look for the positive often enough, we define our life experience.

I'm a very lucky person. As I walk, traffic lights turn green in my favor at crosswalks. I find parking in impossible places and rarely get stuck in traffic. I arrive at the airport, very late, and still make my flight. Things just seem to work out for me, and even when they don't seem to, they eventually turn out fine. While I really do believe myself to be lucky, I also know that it's only true in my own mind. Statistically, I'm just as likely to encounter a red light as I am a green one. Some of the time I find parking, and other times I don't, while my probability of getting stuck in traffic is the same as anyone else's. I've even missed a flight once or twice. But all that doesn't matter! I'm lucky because I notice the green lights more and don't get bothered by the red lights. By choosing where to focus and what to remember, I manufacture my own luck and create a high-quality lifestyle for myself.

We live our stories. All sorts of things happen to us, but our experience is often determined more by the narratives we create around those events rather than by the events themselves. Chris Argyris referred to this process as the Ladder of Inference, where we start with some data, filter it through our observations, weave narratives around those observations, and then finally interpret the narratives into conclusions. Throughout this process we have choices, and the more we choose to emphasize the positive, the happier we are likely to be.

It is our choice, conscious or otherwise, whether to observe and remember the positive occurrences or the negative ones. It is our own minds that then construct stories in order to try and fit the pieces together, and we can tell ourselves whatever stories we want. Too often, we prioritize our predetermined story over any information we might get through our experiences. And finally, as we apply logic to make sense of our stories, we once again choose the connections to make and the standards to apply. By being aware of what we're doing and consciously choosing the positive at any one of these decision points, we can create an optimistic lifestyle and indeed be lucky.

Chapter 55

The Causality Calamity

April 10

> *If you take your beliefs and imagine yourself believing the opposite, you will learn a great deal about your underlying motivations and develop empathy or perspective towards those you currently disagree with.*

Many years ago, I heard of a valley where villagers cultivated their fields using short-handled hoes. All day long, they would work hunched over in the fields, their backs aching from bending down low to turn over the soil. Then, one year, a stranger came by from another area and suggested that if they use long-handled hoes, they could accomplish more, in less time, and with less back pain. The following spring, the villagers switched to long-handled hoes, and enjoyed the benefits, but that summer, the valley was hit with the worst drought in memory, and all of the crops withered. Disgusted, the villagers burned the long-handled hoes, concluding that the change in equipment had brought about the draught, and went back to using short-handled hoes.

We might think this a charming story about a quaint group of people, but how different are we really? What would we have done under those circumstances? How would we have responded if right after switching back to short handles, the rains returned, signaling the end of the drought? Would we be tempted to imagine a causal link between the way we cultivated our fields and the coming of the rain? We might know intellectually that correlation doesn't imply causality, but when faced with coincidences of this nature, our minds want to connect the dots between the unrelated events.

Fear further amplifies our temptation to find connections between things, since we want to bring some predictability to our lives. When bad things happen, we try to explain why, and when good things happen, we want to be able to make them happen again. We wear our lucky hats to sporting events and believe that our plants will grow better if we talk to them. The world is such a confusing place that we try to put some order to it, and while the desire for this is understandable, it is dangerous to imagine causal connections where none exist. We get it wrong much of the time, and our conclusions have consequences.

Every day, we observe the world around us, examine what has come before, and decide what to do next. By drawing invalid conclusions based on assumptions, we make bad decisions, with the potential of harming ourselves and others. We fall prey to our confirmation biases, make judgments bases on our prejudices, and see whatever we want to see. If we fear for our health and believe 5G to be the cause of the pandemic, we might destroy cell phone towers, even if there is no scientific link between the two.

The remedy to this is to be brutally honest with ourselves about what we really know and what we are making up on top of it. Instead of making assumptions, we should look at the evidence, question its sources, examine the methodology, and limit our conclusions to those supported by the data. Knowing that correlation doesn't imply causality is not enough. To make better choices, we must relive this principle every day.

Chapter 56

Thriller

April 17

> *Never say, "things can't get worse," because they can and often will. But they can also get better, and even in a cold, dark, chaotic time, there is room for optimism and hope.*

I don't like scary books and movies. They scare me. While some people are drawn to thrillers, excited by the mystery of not knowing how the story ends and who might get hurt as the tale unfolds, I want to know that everything is going to be okay. I want to know that the people I care about won't get hurt. I want the good guys to win. With books and movies, I can control this to some extent, first by choosing which ones to read or watch, and second, by glancing at the ending before I even open them.

But that is fiction, and reality doesn't quite work that way. In real-life, there is no way of finding out the ending before it happens, and all we can do is spin out the tale as participants or observers and hope for the best. Some people are fine with this, bobbing along the river of time like a turtle on a log, taking in the sights and unconcerned about the future. Others try to control the outcome, swimming this way and that, fighting the current and striving with all their will to determine their own course.

Yet others do a little of both and a lot of neither, peering anxiously at the coming riverbend, fearful of what might be lurking in the unseen future, steering a bit, but feeling helpless to impact the outcome in any significant way. Sadly, that is where I often find myself, reading the news with trepidation, knowing that I'm not going to like a lot of what I read, while also feeling powerless to change the course of events. I'm caught in a thriller, unable to change the channel, and the future remains mysterious to me, and potentially terrifying.

Nearly a year and a half after we started hearing rumors of a new virus, and just over a year since we went into lockdown, the pandemic has turned into a mini-series of thrillers, with each new hopeful development balanced by a new evil plot-twist. At first, we didn't know how bad it was going to be or how to protect ourselves. We cleaned out the world's supply of toilet paper, for some reason, but argued over whether to wear masks. Some questioned the reality of the pandemic, while others got sick and died.

Hotspots emerged, and numbers waxed and waned. While the development of vaccines over the past few months has given us hope that the end of the pandemic might finally be on the horizon, newly mutated variants, more contagious, and deadly, threaten to break through our newly-found immunity. We now seem to be in a race between the latest surge and the vaccines. How many more will get sick and die before this story ends? It's a thriller, and I'm not enjoying it! More than ever, I want to know the end of the story.

Chapter 57

Fifteen Years

April 24

> *Every parting might be forever, and every conversation with someone could be your last. Don't rush off, assuming there will be another day. Let their words linger with you, savor the sound of their voice, the cadence of their breath, and hold their memory close. Your next meeting will be richer for it, and if it never happens, you will have no regrets.*

Since the start of the pandemic, last March, I've written fifty-six articles, but this one, my fifty seventh, will be more personal than most. Fifteen years ago this week, my mother, Aviva Wertheim Cohen, died, succumbing to an illness that had been hanging over her like a death sentence on appeal over a number of years. I feel very fortunate to have had her in my life for over four decades, and while I wish it had been for much longer, I also know that it could have been much shorter as well.

My mother was a courageous optimist, taking on daunting challenges and always looking at the positives. It is from her that I learned to focus more on opportunities than on risks and to believe that even if there's just a small chance of success, that means there's a chance, and it's worth pursuing. To her, optimism was a choice and a habit, and although her life was cut short, her positive outlook allowed her to maintain a high quality of life throughout and to the end. I know where she learned this – her mother, my grandmother, Miriam Simon Wertheim, was the same way. I hope to provide the same example to my kids, students, friends, and colleagues.

Fifteen years is a long time and yet has gone by quickly. It's been a whirlwind of kids, work, and life's opportunities and challenges. I went from being a parent of toddlers and schoolkids to a parent of teens, college students, and adults. My business has grown, I published my first book, and have reinvented myself repeatedly. I've worked with thousands of students and businesspeople all over the world, travelled extensively, and tried to keep everything in balance, as best I could.

So now, fifteen years later, I feel sad that she's been gone so long and that my family, and particularly my father, has been without her company. I cherish the memories we created together and still hear her voice in my mind, reminding me to make lemons out of lemonade and to keep moving forward. More than anything else, I'm grateful to have had the opportunity to learn from her, enjoy her company, and where possible, bring her joy. I'm also thankful for the ways in which her presence and teachings shaped me and made me who I am today.

In our lives, we intersect with many people, some by birth, others by choice, and many by chance. We choose what to take away from these encounters and how to remember them, and every relationship, no matter how short, impacts us in some way, providing us with opportunities to learn things about ourselves, develop our skills, and challenge our mindsets. From my mother, I learned to plan for the future but live in the present. Her experience taught me that our time on the planet might be short, but that our impact can be lasting. Let's keep embracing opportunity and make lemonade!

Chapter 58

Prisoners of Our Nature

May 14

> *The way we measure our success often drives our behavior, so it's important to define our goals thoughtfully. Otherwise, we run the danger of looking back and feeling hollow when we're all done.*

In negotiation classes, the Prisoners' Dilemma is a game that pits groups against each other, giving them the opportunity to collaborate toward a mutual, long-term benefit, or undercut each other, seeking a short-term win and profit-grab. The results typically favor collaboration, encourage risk taking and teach the importance of building trust. Teams that fail to do these things and instead take a competitive approach, trying to profit at the expense of their counterparts, generally produce poorer results for themselves than had they collaborated. While they might "win," in the sense that their counterparts fare even worse, they fail to maximize the value they create for themselves.

And yet, despite this, most of the groups that I've seen play these games fail to realize the full potential of collaboration and frequently fall into very competitive strategies, starting a price war with their counterparts as they race inevitably to the bottom. From the little I know about Game Theory, that result is not unexpected. Our natural impulse is to protect our interests in the short term, and while we compete out of self-defense to avoid risk, in the end, our performance suffers.

As we look at how this plays out in the world around us, we need to look no further than a highway in which a lane has been closed down for construction. A simple lane drop can result in a mile-long backup, driven mostly by aggressive drivers waiting till the last moment to merge into the open lane and stopping everyone in the process. If drivers only worked together, sacrificing a small bit of their advantage and took turns, changing lanes earlier in an orderly fashion, traffic would flow more smoothly and efficiently. But human nature intervenes, and selfish concerns overwhelm the collective benefit.

We see this behavior repeated in many settings. At the start of the pandemic, when we were first confronted by the prospect of being locked down in our homes, we stormed the supermarkets and stocked up on toilet paper, resulting in shortages and empty shelves. It was a crisis driven by human behavior rather than by supply chain, manufacturing, or logistics issues. More recently, the shutdown of the Colonial Pipeline due to a ransomware hack has seen consumers rushing to fill up their tanks, resulting in fuel shortages, long queues, and empty gas stations. Once again, the urge to self-protect and gain personal advantage has resulted in greater pain for all.

We never seem to learn from these examples. Perhaps this kind of selfish, everyone-for-themselves behavior is built into our DNA. We don't want to be the losers who sacrifice our advantage while others leave us in the dust. But as our species multiplies, and the planet gets more crowded, I wonder if we can continue to afford to play out these me-first behaviors, or if learning how to collaborate and work collectively for the common good will be the key to our survival.

Chapter 59

Anxiety Time

May 22

> *Having too much to do can make us very stressed. Having too little to do can also make us stressed. Too much structure in our lives can make us feel hemmed in. Too little structure, and we can feel lost. Each of us has a set of personal Goldilocks zones where we feel "just right" and are at our best, and we need to find our zone!*

Anxiety does weird things to us, and different things to different people. I recently read an article indicating that some people procrastinate not because of poor time management skills, but instead because their emotions get in the way. According to this article, our anxieties over what we have to accomplish shut us down, draining our energy and distracting us from the task at hand.

While I'd never thought of procrastination in these terms, this premise made a lot of intuitive sense to me. How often have I avoided those tasks I found daunting or scary in some way and instead filled my time with other things? I think many of us do this, and only when the scary task has become so urgent that our anxiety of failing at it grows greater than the anxiety of facing it, do we finally attend to it.

Tim Urban talks about procrastination in his TED talk as the struggle between the Instant Gratification Monkey and the Panic Monster. Only when things get really urgent, does the Panic Monster overcome the Instant Gratification Monkey. While some of our instant gratification involves doing things that are more fun or easier than the task at hand, much of our instant gratification involves relief from the anxiety of having to face the task. This would partly explain why some people are more likely to procrastinate than others.

But anxiety has a flipside to it. Some of us, in our anxiety, do everything much earlier than we need to, out of the fear that if we don't, some problem will arise and we won't be able to finish. We arrive at the airport four hours before our flight, preferring to sit by the gate for several hours rather than endure the stress of possibly missing the plane. We plan out everything in our lives to the smallest detail, working from schedules and checklists, believing that if we're not early then we are going to be late.

It's the same anxiety, only with a different face. In either case, we are fearful of the unknown. We don't know how scary the task might be, so we avoid it. We don't know what surprises might await us, so we compensate by preparing for the worst case. While some might argue that one manifestation is better than the other, it might be more helpful to us to examine why we are so anxious.

Life just happens. Many scary tasks turn out to be manageable once we get started, and even the difficult ones, we eventually plod through, and one way or another, get beyond them. Conversely, even the most meticulous planning doesn't save us from having everything go wrong sometimes, and even then, generally, things turn out okay. If, instead, we try to accept the future as inherently unknowable, we might be able to overcome our anxiety and let go of the urge either to avoid it or control it.

Chapter 60

Willpower

May 29

> *If you found out that an asteroid would be hitting the Earth and wiping us out next month, how would you spend your days? If your answer is "exactly as I have been," then your life is truly blessed. If not, imagine how it might be and work toward that goal because some day, the asteroid, or something like it, will be coming.*

There are often things we'd like to change or improve about ourselves. We want to stop procrastinating or conversely, to stop taking on too many obligations, start exercising, eat healthier, or lose weight, keep in touch better or to stop watching so much TV. Each of us has different areas where we try to do better. Sadly, many of these efforts fail to achieve the results we want, or if they do succeed, that success is often temporary. Something happens between idea and execution that derails our progress.

Too often, we either blame ourselves for the failure, citing a lack of willpower, or even if we don't, others look upon us with judgment and do it for us. We, ourselves, do this as well, passing judgment on others as being lazy or weak, equating failure at meeting objectives with character flaws. But adopting a judgmental attitude toward ourselves or others seldom leads to better performance. Instead, it can damage our relationships with others, erodes our self-esteem, and creates a false narrative by which we depict ourselves or others negatively.

The truth is that we don't know why so many of us fail to reach our objectives. It's complicated. Do we need more willpower and determination? Perhaps... Have outside circumstances intervened to derail our progress? Maybe... Are we lacking the skills or infrastructure required to achieve success? Possibly... Are the goals simply unrealistic or beyond our abilities? Could be... Was it bad timing? Who knows... Did we fail to prepare or get the support we needed along the way? Can't be ruled out... The root causes might include any combinations of these and other factors.

While we are often tempted to ascribe a particular cause for the failure, any attempt at a simple explanation is likely to be wrong, or at the very least incomplete. We know so little, and yet purport to have the inside scoop on someone's character and circumstances. This speaks more to our own arrogance, an emotional need to understand the world around us, and lack of empathy toward others. We create stories and then filter our observations through those narratives. Applied to ourselves, our self-judgment reflects an internalization of societal misconceptions and our own disappointment in our perceived failures.

There is nothing wrong with setting lofty, ambitious goals for ourselves and of expecting others to meet their commitments. At the same time, we need to set ourselves and others up for success by ensuring that the infrastructure, skills, preparation, and support are there as well. The work is hard, and success is often elusive, so we need to know when to ask for help and when to offer it to others. We need to be strong and persevere to the best of our abilities, to be resilient and bounce back from setbacks as we can. But in the end, we also need to cut ourselves and others some slack and avoid being simplistic and judgmental.

Chapter 61

After the Apocalypse

June 5

> *Good days pass quickly, and difficult days seem to go on forever, but all that is just perception and illusion. Time flows at the same pace, no matter what we're doing or how we feel, and that is comforting. Good times might last longer than we think, and bad times can end sooner than we expect, so it pays to be positive and hope for the best.*

We've seen this part of the movie before. The flood waters have receded, the bombardment has ended, the storm has passed, or the flames have died down. All is eerily quiet, as people start venturing out into the rubble, first one, then another, and eventually, in large numbers. Initially, no one speaks. People just take it all in – the destruction, the missing neighbors and loved ones, the lost lives, and the missing time. They sift through the rubble, observing small reminders of the world that was before the calamity.

But then, something changes. The survivors start catching each other's eyes, connecting with each other, and greeting each other with hugs, first tentatively, but then with great joy. A feeling of relief at having made it overtakes the survivors, and they turn their backs to the rubble. The celebrations begin, drawing out more people from the shadows, and the scene is awash in jubilation. Too soon, people forget the disaster. Too quickly, they ignore the faint cries of anguish that still emanate from the smoking ruins. They move on and learn nothing, and in their joyous amnesia, set up the sequel of the next apocalypse.

In The Plague, Albert Camus wrote about a city where the Bubonic Plague has broken out. As people sickened, the city was quarantined, sealed off from the world to fight its battle with the deadly disease. The book is a masterpiece, depicting a society under stress, where individuals each try to manage their response to an overwhelming calamity. Like all epidemics, the disease plaguing the city eventually dies out, and the quarantine is lifted. As the gates open, crowds fill the street in joy and jubilation. But one character, Dr. Bernard Rieux, the narrator of the story, who tried to help the townspeople through the plague, does not share in the celebrations. To quote Camus:

"As he listened to the cries of joy rising from the town, Rieux remembered that such joy is always imperiled. He knew what those jubilant crowds did not know but could have learned from books: that the plague bacillus never dies or disappears for good; that it can lie dormant for years and years in furniture and linen-chests; that it bides its time in bedrooms, cellars, trunks, and bookshelves; and that perhaps the day would come when, for the bane and the enlightening of men, it would rouse up its rats again and send them forth to die in a happy city."

Summer is approaching, and many people have been vaccinated. A feeling of relief seems to be sweeping over us, as we emerge from lockdowns and start hugging each other again, dining with friends unmasked, and enjoying our new freedom. But the coronavirus is still out there, biding its time, waiting for opportunities to infect the unwary. We should indeed celebrate, but also remember that it's not over, and try to learn some lessons for the future.

Concluding Thoughts

I hope you enjoyed and got value out of the ideas I shared in these essays. Maybe some made you smile, or think, or do something differently than before. Troubled times happen, and when they strike, we each respond in different ways. One of my responses was to write down my thoughts and share them with others. I found the process both comforting and insightful. It spurred conversations with others, but mostly helped me slow down and be reflective through a challenging year.

The troubles waxed and waned, and now things seem mostly back to normal, but the lessons and ideas endure. Every thought seeds new ideas and creates new opportunities for discussion. I go back and review my words from this past year from time to time. They help be more reflective, more thoughtful, more purposeful in my actions, while also giving me comfort and making me smile. May they accompany you on your journey forward.

Moshe

Index

Choices, Perspective, and Mindfulness

2. The Power of Letting Go, 14
5. Heroes in Small Ways, 20
6. Smart and Lucky, 22
7. Question Everything, 24
8. Humbled and Connected, 26
9. Patience and Perseverance, 28
10. Uncertainty, 30
11. Reach Out Across the Divide, 32
13. Do Something, Anything, 36
14. Summer is Here!, 38
15. Information, Beliefs, and Conclusions, 40
16. Setbacks Happen, 42
17. Life is Good, 44
19. Victory Lap, 48
22. Once Upon a Time, 54
24. Get Lost!, 58
25. What is in the Way?, 60
26. Life is Short, 62
27. Bad Things Happen, 64
29. Out of Our Minds, 68
30. Overwhelmed, 70
31. Yes, We Can, 72
32. The "Uch" Factor, 74
33. Do Something Crazy, 76
34. Everything is Conversation, 78
35. No Easy Answers, 80
36. Life Changing Moments, 82
37. The Marshmallow Test, 84
38. Beyond Marshmallows, 86
39. Every Day, 88

40. Time, 90
41. Resistance to Change, 92
42. Gratitude, 94
43. Happy New Year, 96
44. Curiosity, 98
45. Words Without Consequences, 100
46. Take the Day Off, 102
47. Too Much Bad News, 104
48. A Light in the Distance, 106
49. Judgment Day, 108
50. Lessons from the Weather, 110
51. Jethro the Consultant, 112
52. Milestones, 114
53. Both And, 116
55. The Causality Calamity, 120
56. Thriller, 122
59. Anxiety Time. 128
60. Willpower, 130
61. After the Apocalypse, 132

Connection and Community

4. The Invisible Cocoon, 18
5. Heroes in Small Ways, 20
8. Humbled and Connected, 28
11. Reach Out Across the Divide, 32
12. Hope, Fear and Opportunity, 34
31. Yes, We Can, 72
49. Judgment Day, 108
58. Prisoners of Our Nature, 126

Gratitude and Humility

4. The Invisible Cocoon, 18
8. Humbled and Connected, 28
17. Life is Good, 44
42. Gratitude, 96
57. Fifteen Years, 124

Optimism and Positive Thinking

1. Optimism is a Choice, 12
3. Finding Joy in the Gloom, 16
17. Life is Good, 44
27. Bad Things Happen, 64
43. Happy New Year, 96
47. Too Much Bad News, 104
54. The Optimistic Lifestyle, 118
57. Fifteen Years, 124

Negotiation, Conflict, and Self-Advocacy

18. Negotiating in a Pandemic, 48
20. If We Don't Ask, 50
21. Fear of Conflict, 52
23. Deal or No Deal?, 56
28. Feeling Powerless, 58
34. Everything is Conversation, 78
58. Prisoners of Our Nature, 126

www.ingramcontent.com/pod-product-compliance
Lightning Source LLC
Chambersburg PA
CBHW071246070526
44583CB00017B/2344